mental_floss:

Cocktail Party

Cheat Sheets

Also from **mental**_floss:

mental_floss *presents: Condensed Knowledge*

mental_floss *presents: Forbidden Knowledge*

mental_floss *presents: Instant Knowledge*

mental_floss: *Scatterbrained*

mental_floss: *What's the Difference?*

mental_floss: *The Genius Instruction Manual*

mental_floss:

Cocktail Party

Cheat Sheets

edited by Will Pearson, Mangesh Hattikudur, and John Green

Collins

An Imprint of HarperCollinsPublishers

HarperCollins books may be purchased for educational, business, or sales promotional use. For information, please write: Special Markets Department, HarperCollins Publishers, 10 East 53rd Street, New York, NY 10022.

FIRST EDITION

Designed by Emily Cavett Taff

Library of Congress Cataloging-in-Publication Data has been applied for.

ISBN-10: 0-06-088251-4
ISBN-13: 978-0-06-088251-8

06 07 08 09 10 WBC/RRD 10 9 8 7 6 5 4 3 2 1

Dedication

John

Ilene Cooper, who edited my first book, helped me court the woman who became my wife, and taught me everything I know about the Dead Sea Scrolls, book reviewing, and Liza Minnelli's ex-husbands.

Mangesh

To my cousin Sonal, who refuses to visit the United States, but I still love anyway.

Will

To my sister, who had the idea to do this book because she couldn't keep her facts straight after a couple cocktails.

"I just use my muscles as a conversation piece,
like someone walking a cheetah down
Forty-second Street."

—Arnold Schwarzenegger

Contents

Introduction

INTRODUCTION

Each December, the staff of *mental_floss* gathers for our "Genghis Khan Is Dead" Cocktail Party. The GKID Cocktail Party was originally known as the Christmas Party, until it came to our attention that many members of our staff do not celebrate Christmas, causing us to rename it the Holiday Party. But that didn't mollify some folks, either because they didn't celebrate any holidays in December or because they were generally opposed to merriment. So, for a while, we just called it the Winter Event, but then one of our resident science nerds argued that associating winter with December alienates all those who live in the southern hemisphere and experience winter in June. So, finally, we decided to celebrate Genghis Khan's death, because (1) he's dead, and (2) everybody agreed he was a jerk.

At *mental_floss*, our cocktail parties are all about sounding (and, to a lesser extent, being) smart. If you can't hold your conversational own, you're in trouble.

And at the most recent GKID Cocktail Party, as it happens, I could not hold my own. I mistook my Thomas Hobbes for my John Locke. I confused my martinis and my vodka martinis. I found myself half-remembering great witticisms, but failing to recall if they were originally spoken by Samuel Johnson, or

Mark Twain, or Confucius. Admittedly, this had something to do with the boozing. But on a deeper level, I just couldn't skate through intellectual conversations the way cocktail partiers need to.

And so this book was born.

Our aim here is to take a variety of topics you (and I) sort of halfway hazily remember, and give you all the knowledge you need to survive even the most rigorous cocktail party conversation.

Now, you won't find any tips and tricks on how to discuss celebrity breakups, the weather, or recent movies, which we realize are all common cocktail party topics. We trust that you can fake your way through those conversations. But should Joan of Arc come up, we want you to feel every bit as comfortable discussing her wacky antics as you do chatting about those of Britney Spears.

In addition to all the basic information you'll need on a topic, we've collected handy conversation starters—because really, what fun is it to know a lot about the *Kama Sutra* if you can't wedge your expertise into conversation? And we've included helpful pronunciation guides, because nothing endears you to cocktail party acquaintances quite like correcting their pronunciation of W. E. B. Du Bois. Plus, we'll tell you about some cocktail party situations where it will be appropriate to drop your knowledge.

I feel confident I'm going to rock next year's GKID Cocktail Party—and so can you. (Well, assuming you can swing an invitation. J. Lo wanted to come last year but the *mental_floss* brass was all, like, "Sorry, but Diddy's coming and that could be really awkward.") Our sincere hope is that you'll never again have to worry about sounding like a fool at a party—unless, that is, you fail to keep your martini consumption in check.

Which reminds me of something Dorothy Parker once said: "I like to have a martini / Two at the very most. / Three, I'm under the table / Four, I'm under the host." (See how it works?!)

—*John Green*

mental_floss:
Cocktail
Party

Cheat Sheets

Alexander the Great

Name-dropping: Alexander (pronunciation: um, obvious) (356–323 BCE). Noted emperor who once ruled half the world despite never seeing his 34th birthday. Alexander's biggest regret? Not living long enough to forcibly capture the state of California and prevent Oliver Stone from making a wretched biopic of his life.

When to Drop Your Knowledge: Knowledge of Alexander will come in handy if you ever find yourself at a cocktail party with Oliver Stone. Also, when the party goes late and most people have gone home and you and your friends sit around and try to think of ways to take over the world, your strategizing might benefit from knowledge of the Master.

The Basics

He lived his life, and fought his wars, more like the game of Risk than anyone before or since: Find an army, beat it, leave a couple board pieces to protect your flank, and move on. Alexander the Great to most, to the Persians he was simply Alexander the Please Stop Conquering Us.

The son of Greek emperor Philip II, Alexander grew up under the tutelage of no less a teacher than Aristotle. (In a characteristic act of ingratitude, Alexander later ordered the execution of Aristotle's nephew.) He assumed the throne at age

Death of a Macedonian

Alexander died in 323 BCE, at the age of 33. Almost from the beginning, rumors persisted that he was poisoned to death, either by his enemies or his wife. The poisoning theory gained credence because shortly before he became seriously ill, Alexander felt a stabbing pain in his liver after drinking wine (which is generally called a hangover). For centuries, most historians thought a relapse of malaria was to blame for Alexander's death. But in a 1998 study, pathologist David W. Oldach diagnosed Alexander's fatal illness as typhoid, possibly complicated by Guillain-Barré syndrome, in which the immune system attacks the nervous system. Oddly enough, Guillain-Barré often causes paralysis, leading to the disconcerting possibility that Alexander *was* murdered after all—by his embalmers as he lay in a state of complete immobility.

20, and when some Greek cities were slow to swear allegiance to him, he ordered the execution of all his rivals to the throne and then marched off to ensure his control of all Greece.

Alexander enjoyed marching through Greece so much that he went on to invade the Persian Empire. By 332 BCE, he had "liberated" all of Persia and Egypt. His army was the best trained in the world at the time, and he employed a huge cavalry force along with Special Teams Forces–like bands of commandos who attacked at night with javelins. (Although they are now primarily utilized in a universally unwatched Olympic sport, javelins were once considered top-notch weapons.)

After 10 years of constant conquering, Alexander had nearly reached the Ganges River in India when his soldiers decided they were tired and wanted to go home.

They mutinied, and although Alexander had the leaders of the rebellion executed, he was sympathetic to his soldiers, forgave most of them, and agreed to stop fighting—at least for a while. Fortunately for the soldiers and unfortunately for Alexander, the Great Emperor died soon after going to Babylon to regroup and solidify his empire.

Probably the greatest general of antiquity, Alexander was also capable of blind cruelty. He ordered countless executions and preferred invasion to negotiation. But he was also the first great multiculturalist: After conquering the Persian Empire, he adopted Persian dress and many of their customs, and even staged a mass wedding at which his soldiers were married off to (rather unwilling) Persian girls.

Good to Know . . .

Alexander's epitaph is one of the most famous in history: "A tomb now suffices him for whom the whole world was not sufficient." But in all likelihood, Alexander's tomb does not contain Alexander himself. The emperor Ptolemy took Alexander's body and brought it to Alexandria, where it was on display for a long time. But the body was eventually lost, and its current whereabouts is unknown.

Conversation Starters

◆ W. H. Cobb was a state senator and armchair historian in 19th-century Georgia who'd been reading about Alexander's attack on the city of Tyre when his first son was born in 1886. He thought so highly of the Phoenicians' tenacity in the face of Alexander's attack that he gave his son the unusual name Tyrus. Ty Cobb would go on to be every bit as fierce and nasty as the citizens of Tyre.

◆ It's well known that Alexander today would be considered bisexual, although in antiquity, same-sex attraction was considered universal and thought to be entirely customary. Alexander's closest relationship, which most historians think had a sexual facet, was with his cavalry commander Hephaestion. He and Hephaestion were so close that when his pal died of an illness, a grief-stricken Alexander did the only thing he could do to cheer himself up: He waged an extermination campaign against the nearest enemy he could find (the unlucky victims were the Cossaens).

◆ According to the "historian" Plutarch (you'll understand the ironic quotes in just a moment), Phillip II wasn't *really* Alexander's father. Phillip, Plutarch wrote, feared Alexander's mom Olympias because she apparently liked to sleep with snakes. But there was one Ancient Greek who'd sleep with any woman under any circumstances: Zeus. Plutarch goes on to relay that Zeus impregnated Olympias with his trademark thunder-and-lightning technique, making her son Alexander half-man and half-god.

Attila the Hun

Name-dropping: Attila (pronunciation: uh-TILL-uh) (406–453 CE). Nicknamed Flagellum Dei, Latin for "the Scourge of God," he was the last king of the Huns in Europe, a brilliant general with a deep and abiding fondness for killing people.

Huns: Originally referring to east Asian nomads, the name came to refer to any nomads from central Asia (now known, colloquially, as "the 'Stans"), including those who rose to prominence in eastern Europe during the last days of the Roman Empire.

When to Drop Your Knowledge: Well, it's must-have material if your cocktail party happens to get attacked by a gang of barbarians or possibly Cure-embracing goths. But Attila the Hun is also great joke fodder anytime you're drinking a Bloody Mary. When someone asks what you're drinking, you just say, "In the great tradition of Attila the Hun, I'm drinking the blood of my children! Ha-ha!" That's comic gold.

The Basics

By the turn of the fifth century, the Roman Empire was in trouble due to poor leadership, gluttony at home, and an overextended military. (Sure, it sounds familiar, but we don't make those jokes, because this is an apolitical book.) Large swaths of the Roman Empire were ripe for the picking, but, as the world's only superpower, the Romans had only to fear periodic revolts among the lesser barbarians (see sidebar).

Barbarians

Barbarian: Originally a Greek term referring to any kind of non-Greek. The Romans used the word to describe any foreigners who wanted to attack them. So attacks from "barbarians" came in many types, including . . .

Visigoths. Western Goths, who once ruled much of contemporary Spain and France. The Visigoths practiced Arianism, which sounds racist but is actually just a branch of Christianity that denies Jesus' place in the Trinity.

The Eastern Goths. Called Ostrogoths, they were somewhat less unfriendly toward the Roman Empire, though they still sacked some cities when the mood struck.

Vandals—It was the Vandals from northern Europe who sacked Rome in 455. The Vandals took treasures from the Temple of Jerusalem, countless valuables, and even the empress, who was imprisoned in Carthage for seven years.

But then came Attila. The nephew of Rua, who'd united the Hun tribes from central Asia to eastern Europe, Attila inherited the throne in 434 CE. There was only one problem: Attila had to share power with his older brother, Bleda. He and Bleda immediately set off to conquer large parts of the Persian Empire. But the Persians defeated the Huns in Armenia. The loss was chalked up to mere practice, and life went on (at least for the surviving Huns).

In 440, claiming that the Romans weren't paying the Huns adequate tribute in gold, the Brothers Hun attacked the Roman Empire. Over the next five years, they stampeded through the Balkans, across the Danube, and made it all the way to the gates of Constantinople. In 443, they negotiated a very favorable truce with the Roman Empire, and then Attila decided to go home for a while so as to kill his brother and take full control of the rest of the Huns.

Which is precisely what Attila did in 445. By 451, Attila began one of the largest invasions in history, using some 500,000 men to attack Gaul, present-day France. Then in 452, he turned to the Italian peninsula, the heart of the empire itself. He ravaged the countryside for months before the Pope convinced him not to attack Rome itself. With huge chunks of Asia and Europe in his command, it seemed that Attila might found the new great superpower. But then he died. Of a nosebleed. (See sidebar.)

And his empire died with him. Attila's three surviving sons caused endless internal power struggles and none of them had the political or military shrewdness of their father. The Hunnish Empire faded in significance. Rome, on the other hand, staggered on for a few more decades.

DEATH OF A HUN

On the last night of his life, Attila was up partying to celebrate his marriage to Ildikó, a superhot Goth. Although Attila didn't usually drink, the 47-year-old king proceeded to get trashed. Attila passed out, suffered a nosebleed in his sleep, and then pulled a variation on the Hendrix by choking to death—on his own blood. It's one of those stories too odd to be made up, and most scholars believe in its historicity. But a few have argued that Attila was murdered—possibly by his new wife, and possibly by political enemies (of whom, goodness knows, he had plenty).

Conversation Starters

◆ While generally reviled as a barbarian in the West, Attila is a national hero in eastern Europe and central Asia. In both Hungary and Turkey, "Attila" is a popular name for boys, and girls are often named after Attila's last wife, Ildikó.

◆ Although Attila started a lot of wars over gold, he didn't care much about the finer things. He ate from a wooden plate, drank from a wooden cup, and apparently ate nothing but meat.

◆ Like Mickey Rooney, Lana Turner, and Elizabeth Taylor, Attila married more than six different people.

◆ Many sources claim Attila was a semifrequent cannibal, which—while certainly not impossible—was a charge usually leveled by enemy historians. But the most damning charge is that Attila committed the double taboo of *incestuous* cannibalism, which is so gross we can hardly even think about it. Supposedly, Attila's wife killed two of his sons in retribution for the murder of her brothers. And then she cooked the kids and served them to Attila, claiming they were a rare and tender meat. (Which, technically, we suppose, was not a lie.)

Augustine

Name-dropping: Augustine (pronunciation: uh-GUS-tin if you're trying to impress people; AW-guh-steen if you're talking about the town in Florida) (354–430 CE). The most important Christian theologian ever, except for St. Paul, whose thoughts on God ended up filling out the latter half of the New Testament. St. Augustine didn't get so lucky—but he still gets read by anyone seriously studying the Christian understanding of God.

When to Drop Your Knowledge: Augustine is sure to add heft to those late-night religion debates. But more important: He authored one of the greatest pickup lines in history, which works today just as nicely as it worked in 400 CE.

The Basics

Born in Africa (in what is now Algeria), Augustine was raised a Christian but left behind the blessed life when he began attending school in Carthage, which was sort of the fourth century's South Padre Island: spring break all year round. In his youth, Augustine fathered an illegitimate son, but by the age of 21, he began to get serious about spirituality. He undertook a deep and serious study of philosophy, theology, and religion while teaching school in Milan—and then, on Easter Day in the year 387, Augustine was baptized a Christian. The Church would never be the same.

Manichaeans

Pop Quiz: What's the name of the religious doctrine founded by a charismatic fellow who believed in baptism and ended up getting crucified? Why, Manichaeism, of course. Founded in the third century by a Persian named Mani who was eventually crucified for his beliefs, Manichaeism stressed the duality of good and evil and claimed to have successfully synthesized all the world's major religions. Although Manichaeism survived in Turkey and the Middle East until after 1000 CE, it was eventually overtaken by Islam and Christianity. We're just grateful Mel Gibson isn't a Manichaean, because as gory as his *Passion of the Christ* is, Mani's story is even worse: After being crucified in 276 by a Persian emperor, Mani's body was flayed, gutted, stuffed, and hung up at the city gates as a warning to his followers.

A mere eight years after his conversion, he was bishop of Hippo (the Algerian city, not the Hungry Hungry board game icon), a position he held for the rest of his career. Although said to be an unusually good preacher, Augustine made his real mark with his writing by making his outlandishly complicated theology comprehensible to a lay audience better than anyone has since. *On the Trinity* did more to define the Christian understanding of the Trinity than any church council. And *City of God,* which we recommend reading if you have seven or eight free years, is a sprawling and beautiful defense of Christianity against paganism that is so incredibly and utterly long that many people have converted to Christianity just so they wouldn't have to keep reading it.

From the beginning, the Catholic Church embraced Augustine's work. But his radical emphasis on grace as the means to salvation would later

The Quotable Augustine

And now for the pickup line! In his memoir *Confessions*, Augustine recounts that he would pray, "Lord, make me chaste—but not yet." As Augustine well knew, this works great as a pickup line. Nothing makes someone feel special like you ripping off your habit or priestly collar and saying, "Lord, make me chaste—but not yet."

Here are some Augustine quotes (that aren't pickup lines) that might one day come in handy.

When you're asked a difficult question: "What then is time? If no one asks me, I know what it is. If I wish to explain it to him who asks, I do not know."

When musing on war: "The purpose of all wars is peace."

When explaining to your children how reality television got popular: "Miracles are not contrary to nature, only to what we know about nature."

inspire the likes of Martin Luther and John Calvin when they were asserting that faith alone leads to heaven. So, basically, everyone loved Augustine. Except of course the Manicheans, whom he helped destroy.

Conversation Starters

◆ Because Augustine's work was immediately considered so significant, a *lot* of his writing has survived—about 5,000,000 words, in fact. (That's approximately 100 of these books.)

◆ There's a pervasive rumor that St. Augustine invented the phrase "missionary position." This is simply untrue. (However, there are vague statements in Augustine's writing that imply he believed the missionary position was the least sinful.) So where did the phrase "missionary position" come from? Its first use appears to have been in about 1969—probably by some counterculture kids who were ridiculing the position as boring and prudish.

◆ Augustine is so important that his *mom* got sainted (she's St. Monica), mostly for doing such an excellent job raising him. Augustine's dad, on the other hand, is not a saint. He is remembered primarily for cheating on St. Monica.

◆ Augustine is called one of the "Four Great Fathers of the Latin Church," but that's a little like saying that all four Beatles were created equal. Of the Four Fathers (the other three are the less-great and less-famous Jerome, Ambrose, and Gregory the Great), Augustine's importance far outstrips the others. He's Paul *and* John—so Augustine's the only fourth-century name you need to drop.

Beethoven

Name-dropping: Ludwig van Beethoven (pronunciation: BAY-toh-ven if you're not watching *Bill and Ted's Excellent Adventure*; BEETH-uh-ven if you are) (1770–1827). World-famous composer whose songs we often find ourselves humming because they're prominently featured in that one hearing aid battery commercial. Man, Beethoven is such a sellout.

When to Drop Your Knowledge: You're at a quiet, staid cocktail party. A sonata plays in the background, but not too loudly. Everyone's too dressed up, and no one seems to know what to talk about. How can you make this party *fun?* Well, remind people that Beethoven wasn't always background music. He was revolutionary, and thrilling! And also he was totally nuts. And once you get people started *talking* about crazy, they'll feel more comfortable *getting* a little crazy.

The Basics

Ludwig van Beethoven was one of those geniuses who bolster the stereotype that with genius comes insanity and cruelty. He was often observed walking through the streets of Vienna wearing ratty clothes, humming off-key to himself, and scribbling his thoughts into a notebook. Impulsive and often quite cruel, Beethoven wasn't as likable as his music.

But he had a hard life. He never fared well with the ladies (after one courtship failed, he contemplated suicide), he was

Quotes by and About Beethoven

Beethoven's Ninth Symphony proved to be his last, which is a surprisingly common phenomenon among composers. Both Schubert and Dvořák died before composing a Tenth Symphony as well. Mahler, a notoriously superstitious fellow, tried to buck the trend by hurrying through his Tenth Symphony, but died with it unfinished anyway. Finnish composer Jean Sibelius, meanwhile, retired after his Eighth Symphony, and survived another 33 years.

On music: "Music is the mediator between spiritual and sensual life."

On having a high opinion of one's self: "What you are, you are by accident of birth; what I am, I am by myself. There are and will be a thousand princes; there is only one Beethoven."

On soup: "Anyone who tells a lie has not a pure heart, and cannot make a good soup." (We told you he was crazy.)

the product of an abusive home, and, of course, his one true love was music, which makes life hard when you start going deaf at the age of 28. Imagine if Michael Jackson woke up at the age of 28 and suddenly could no longer dance or sing or write songs. Oh, wait. That happened. And look at the results!

Beethoven's career is usually broken down into three parts. In his early career, he wrote his first and second symphonies, where you still find the lingering influence of past composers like Haydn and Mozart. Despite the fact that he still had his hearing, and he'd written the famous *Pathetique Sonata* during it, the early part of Beethoven's career is generally held to be his least artistically important. Beethoven's middle period began just after the earth-shattering news of his deafness and lasted 20 years. Still, he managed to compose

> **Beethoven on Beethoven:** "Beethoven can write music, thank God, but he can do nothing else on earth."
>
> **Eddie Van Halen on Beethoven:** "Some people think a song without words isn't a real song. Tell that to Beethoven and he'll kick your a**!"

six symphonies, dozens of piano sonatas, and his only opera, *Fidelio*.

It was the last ten years of his professional career, however, that saw the works most admired today. Although by now he was *totally* deaf, Beethoven's late period saw the composition of his great Ninth Symphony (the one that features that brilliant and catchy "Ode to Joy"). Of course, simply remembering Ludwig as the deaf composer doesn't do the guy justice. Beethoven's career straddled the fence between Classicism and Romanticism in classical music, and few have ever matched the intellectual heft of his compositions.

A SOUND ARGUMENT

The argument over the cause of Beethoven's loss of hearing has been raging since back when Beethoven could actually listen (albeit through an ear trumpet) to people fighting over it. The loss may have been due to direct damage to the arterial nerve, thickening of the bones in the middle ear, or the alcoholism that caused him to suffer hepatitis.

Conversation Starters

◆ Beethoven's Ninth was commissioned by the Philharmonic Society of London (Beethoven was paid 100 pounds for it). When he delivered the composition, the Philharmonic deemed it beautiful but absolutely impossible to play. For decades, in fact, many orchestras just skipped the hard parts.

◆ For 170 years, everyone agreed that Beethoven, who drank too much for much of his life and suffered the symptoms of hepatitis for a decade before his death, died of liver failure. But a four-year analysis of a lock of Beethoven's hair beginning in 1996 showed that Beethoven seemed to suffer from acute lead poisoning that likely caused his death. The lead poisoning may have been caused by purportedly health-restoring mineral water he drank while staying at health spas.

◆ Beethoven often gave improvisational concerts to audiences of aristocratic patrons and their friends. People found these events so moving that they often burst into tears. After he finished playing one such concert, Beethoven laughed at the tear-stained faces in the audience and said, "You fools! Who can live among such children?" How terribly, um, grown-up of him.

Beowulf

Name-dropping: *Beowulf* (pronunciation: BAY-oh-wuhlf) (written between 700 and 1000 CE). The italicized *Beowulf* is an epic poem, apparently written in English (although you wouldn't know that to read it). The nonitalicized Beowulf is the poem's hero, a knight-in-shining-armor type.

Grendel (pronunciation: GREN-dul): A horrible monster.

When to Drop Your Knowledge: Whenever you find yourself chatting with a pretentious one-time English major (you can spot them by the repeated references to Proust and the suit jacket with elbow patches). But *Beowulf* will also give you a tale to tell while you drink an actual Grendel, a lemonade-based, liqueur-stuffed, sticky-sweet cocktail.

The Basics

Beowulf is widely considered to be the first great work of literature in English—even though all the words are spelled weird, as if its author (whose identity is unknown) was hooked on phonics. The language is so inaccessible, in fact, that many translations have been published (most notably, Nobel Prize winner Seamus Heaney's, in 2001). *Beowulf* is the epic story of a fellow named, well, Beowulf. It is told in two parts.

Part 1: A horrible monster named Grendel has, for 12 years, attacked a Danish mead hall every single night, plucking

MEAD

Whether it's a bodice-ripping romance set in the dark ages or *Beowulf* itself, everybody in 10th-century Europe seems to be drinking mead. So what is the stuff? It's a sweet wine, fermented from honey, and its history dates back to 2000 BCE—when the Babylonians used to lap it up. With a reputation for being wickedly strong, you'd think it'd be popular today, but grape wine is a far more palatable taste. Still, if you're keen on getting your hands around a flagon of the good stuff, you can probably pick some up at a Renaissance Faire. (And no, we won't own up to how we know that!)

Although most of *Beowulf* is obviously made up, some details are historically accurate. Hygelac, the Danish king in Part 1 of *Beowulf*, really did die around 516 CE while leading a Viking raid into the Netherlands, just as *Beowulf* recounts. A fire-spitting dragon, however, did not show up in Denmark a few years later.

drinkers from their seats and killing them. Frankly, you'd think they could just close down that mead hall that Grendel so hates and open up another one farther down the street. But regardless, a young prince named Beowulf arrives on the scene and promises to save the mead drinkers from their evil monster. That very night, Grendel shows up, eats a sleeping man, and then runs into Beowulf. Our hero valiantly battles the evil Grendel, eventually tearing off his arm. Grendel manages to escape, but the wound proves fatal. Beowulf is widely lauded for his bravery and strength, but the troubles aren't over.

The next evening, Grendel's mom (even monsters have mothers) shows up and demands wergild, a form of medieval payment to make up for the killing of a relative. The mead drinkers refuse, no doubt wondering where *their* wergild is for

Grendel's 12-year murderous rampage. Enraged, Grendel's mother kills a man. The next morning, Beowulf gets up, tracks Grendel's mother to a cave, decapitates her, and returns home with her head, whereupon the mead flows in earnest.

Part 2: Many years later, Beowulf has been king for a tranquil 50 years when a fire-breathing dragon shows up. The dragon's carnage puts Grendel to shame, and Beowulf is older and weaker now, but he still summons the will to fight. After a bitter battle, Beowulf succeeds in killing the dragon, but not before he himself is mortally wounded. The epic ends with Beowulf's somber funeral.

Most critics see the story of Beowulf as a Christian allegory—Beowulf stands up to the forces of evil, and in the end sacrifices himself for the good of the world. Besides that, it's a rip-roaring adventure story. Sure, "English" like "swa mec gelome laðgeteonan/þreatedon þearle," makes it a wee inaccessible—but that's why you've got cheat sheets. (Translation, by the way: "Me thus often the evil monsters/thronging threatened.")

Conversation Starters

◆ *Lord of the Rings* author and weird-language nut J.R.R. Tolkien was fascinated by *Beowulf*—he often wrote about it and even wrote an unpublished translation. *Beowulf* was an important inspiration for Tolkien's own epic, and much of the made-up languages in his books bear the imprint of Old English. The *Rings'* antagonist Saruman, for instance, gets his name from the Old English word for treachery.

◆ With a total of 3,182 lines, *Beowulf* is the longest Old English manuscript in existence. In fact, it comprises about a tenth of all Anglo-Saxon poetry known to still exist. But it's not the oldest poem in English: That distinction goes to Caedmon's "Hymn of Creation," which—believe us—isn't famous for a reason.

◆ Only a single original manuscript of *Beowulf* survives, and it was severely damaged in a fire in 1731 while in storage at a place called the "Ashburnham House." Just goes to show you that one ought not store a priceless, one-of-a-kind epic poem at a joint containing both the words "ash" and "burn" in its name.

◆ The world of Beowulf also attracted a somewhat dimmer literary light. Novelist Michael Crichton, so rich he won't mind us calling him a hack, wrote a book called *Eaters of the Dead* (later made into the movie *The 13th Warrior*) that imagined the Beowulf story through the eyes of a 10th-century Muslim. In Crichton's account, "Grendel" is not a regular monster but, well, a tribe of Neanderthal cannibals.

Simón Bolívar

Name-dropping: Simón Bolívar (pronunciation: see-MOAN bo-LEE-varr—and remember to roll those r's) (1783–1830). South American revolutionary who brought independence to much of the continent but gets absolutely no props, while Che (freaking) Guevera, who never liberated anybody, gets his face plastered all over hipsters' T-shirts.

When to Drop Your Knowledge: Well, whenever you see a Che shirt, for starters. But you can also use your knowledge of Bolívar to impress students of colonialism, revolutionaries, American Civil War buffs, and fans of South American author Gabriel García Márquez.

The Basics

Known as "The Liberator," Simón Bolívar came from a wealthy Venezuelan family. He studied in Europe, married the daughter of a prominent Spaniard (sadly, Bolívar's wife died soon after of yellow fever), and received an excellent education from private tutors. But by his 21st birthday, Bolívar began to imagine a South America free from colonialism and, in typically dramatic fashion, stood atop a mountain in Rome and made a solemn vow to liberate his homeland.

Plenty of kids in their early 20s have big ideas, but Bolívar made it happen. With Spain weak due to Napoléon's invasions, Bolívar began leading Latin American independence move-

Bolívar's Labyrinth

The tragic last months of Simón Bolívar's life are recounted to brilliant effect in Nobel Laureate Gabriel García Márquez's 1981 novel *The General in His Labyrinth*. In the book, "The General" vacillates between an acceptance that he is near death and a fierce determination to begin a revolution anew. García Márquez's version of Bolívar's last words is particularly moving. In the midst of a hellish fever, The General wakes up and says, "Damn it. How will I ever get out of this labyrinth?" it seems that Bolívar *did* indeed ask that question, but it wasn't his final utterance. His real *last* words were likely the more pedestrian "José, bring the baggage."

ments. And despite his initially failing to win independence for Venezuela, his forces eventually prevailed, entering Caracas in 1813. It was then that Bolívar began a long and storied tradition in Latin American politics by immediately declaring himself president of Venezuela, by which he meant "dictator."

It was Bolívar's dream that all Latin America would be a single giant nation (and he also dreamed, no doubt, of running it himself). In the next few years, it seemed he might accomplish it. One by one, territories were brought into the fold of "Gran Colombia." Besides Venezuela, Bolívar helped to liberate Ecuador, Peru, Colombia, Bolivia (naturally), and Panama. But Bolívar's dream was never terribly realistic. Internal factionalism caused him constant problems and left him frequently out of power, and his unrepentant lust for power (he wrote a constitution for Gran Colombia that made him president for life and gave him the ability to choose a successor) made him unpopular in spite of all he'd done to bring sovereignty to South America.

Name Game

Simón Bolívar is the only person in the world to have not one, but *two*, sovereign nations named after him: Bolivia and Venezuela. Before you try to find the "Venezuela" in Bolívar's full name, allow us to explain. It turns out that the full name of Venezuela is "Bolivarian Republic of Venezuela." (Additionally, he's also got a square in Egypt named after him, as well as the official currency of Venezuela, the bolívar.)

He resigned his presidency of Gran Colombia once and for all in 1830, after spending the latter part of his career trying to quell uprisings throughout South America. Suffering from tuberculosis, he spent the last six months of his life adrift, still vaguely dreaming of a powerful, united South America. Simón died of tuberculosis on December 17, 1830. A great general who lusted too much for power, his faults have largely been forgotten today, and although he is not as famous as he ought to be in the U.S., Bolívar is revered throughout much of South America.

Conversation Starters

◆ Simón Bolívar had one of the most impressive full names in all of human history: Simón José Antonio de la Santísima Trinidad Bolívar y Palacios.

◆ We've often pondered why it is, exactly, that Goofy, a dog, gets to be Mickey Mouse's zany, talkative pal, while Pluto, also a dog, is merely Mickey's pet. And it's hard not to feel sorry for poor, mute Pluto. But it turns out that Pluto has a comrade. Donald Duck's pet dog, Bolivar (who was indeed named for Simón), first appeared in Disney cartoons in 1938. Like Pluto, he can't talk and always walks on four legs. How typical of The Man to name a hapless, mute mutt after a brilliant South American general.

◆ It wasn't just South America that revered Bolivar. Although it may be hard to imagine a Southerner named for a Venezuelan revolutionary, there was indeed at least one such man: Simon Bolivar Buckner Sr., a mustachioed Kentuckian, was a lieutenant general in the Confederate Army during the American Civil War. After the war, he served as governor of Kentucky.

He wasn't embarrassed by the name, either. In fact, he passed it on to his son, Simon Bolivar Buckner Jr., who also became a general, but this time in the U.S. army. An unrepentant racist who refused to lead African-American troops, Junior nonetheless commanded the assault on Okinawa. He was killed by artillery fire during the battle, making him the highest-ranking American soldier to die in World War II.

The Brontës

Name-dropping: Charlotte (1816–1855), Emily (1818–1848), and Anne Brontë (1820–1849) (pronunciation: BRON-tay, but more on that later). A trio of sisters from Yorkshire, England, whose brilliantly imagined novels shook up Victorian literature and have been a staple of 19th-century literature classes ever since.

When to Drop Your Knowledge: Whenever you find yourself drinking with a student of 19th-century literature, you'll need all the Brontës you can muster. But knowledge of the Brontës will also come in handy if you get stuck listening to a boring, nostalgic tale of the halcyon days of yore. Just cut them off and say, "I'm sure the holiday parties/red wine/sporting events were better in the old days. But in the old days, no one got to enjoy any of it, because everyone was constantly dying of tuberculosis."

The Basics

The Brontë sisters were close growing up. They attended boarding school together, and watched their sisters Maria and Elizabeth die of tuberculosis in their childhood. Eventually, they would all share the same fate.

CHARLOTTE

The oldest of the three, Charlotte wrote four novels, but it was her first, *Jane Eyre*, that's become a classic. The story of a young

The Unfortunate Mr. Branwell Brontë

When the Brontë siblings were children, the girls were thought bright—but not near so talented as young Branwell Brontë, the lone boy. His one literary contribution—an unpublished translation of Horace—was supposedly admired by Samuel Taylor Coleridge. (Branwell had something else in common with Coleridge: They were both fond of opium.) The clear black sheep of the family, Branwell got fired from the only two jobs he ever had (once for sleeping with the boss's wife), and eventually returned home. While his sisters wrote, he spent his days drinking and smoking opium. In the end, he became so strung out that it's not known for sure whether he ever learned of his sisters' success. Regardless, soon after the Brontë girls became literary celebrities, Branwell died of— that's right—tuberculosis.

governess in love with a man who has a secret (and very crazy) wife chained in his attic, *Jane Eyre* wasn't well received by critics, but it sold well from the beginning, and—as is so often the case—the critics ended up looking foolish. Charlotte married at 37; she was pregnant a year later when she died suddenly, apparently of tuberculosis.

EMILY

The middle sister, Emily was the quietest of the sisters, but today she's generally considered the most talented. Her early poems show a talent for verse, and her lone novel, *Wuthering Heights*, is stylistically dazzling. It contains stories within stories, a reading experience that has been compared to opening a matryoshka doll. But Emily did not live to write another book. Shortly after the publication of *Wuthering Heights*, she caught tuberculosis. A few months later, she died at the age of 30.

Extra Credit:
TB

Something about 19th-century writers—their depressive dispositions, perhaps—seemed to attract death by tuberculosis. Besides the Brontës, Robert Louis Stevenson, D. H. Lawrence, and Anton Chekov all died of TB. Perhaps the most tragic death was that of John Keats, the outlandishly promising British poet who died in 1821 at the tender age of 25. Keats remained a brilliant poet to his bitter end. His last will and testament, one perfect line of iambic pentameter, was also his last poem: "My chest of books divide amongst my friends."

ANNE

Let's not sugarcoat it. Compared to her sisters, Anne was something of a hack. Pious, quiet, and perhaps too traditional for her own good, Anne's most famous novel, *Agnes Grey*, is a mediocre example of the "governess novel" (the 19th-century equivalent of *The Nanny Diaries*). Still, Anne was only 28 when her second novel was published, and she might have gone on to match her sisters' brilliance. But she caught—you guessed it—tuberculosis. She died at the age of 29.

WHATEVER RINGS YOUR BELL

All three Brontë sisters wrote for most of their lives under gender-ambiguous pseudonyms. Charlotte was Currer Bell; Emily, Ellis Bell; and Anne, Acton Bell. Many 19th-century women (most famously George Eliot) used pseudonyms, because critics and reviewers expected women to write prim-and-proper books. In retrospect, most of the great 19th-century British novelists were women—and none of them wrote merely proper novels.

Conversation Starters

◆ If Brontë seems like an odd name for a middle-class British family, well—it is. The Brontës' father was an Anglican minister named Patrick Brunty. But the good Rev. Brunty thought his name sounded painfully unsophisticated, so he changed it—several times. First, it was Branty, then Bronte, and then Bronté, before he finally settled on the Brontë.

◆ Incidentally, the accent mark in Brontë is known as a *diaeresis*, which is a word that frankly contains too many vowels to ever become popular. A diaeresis indicates that a vowel should be pronounced. Although extremely rare today, it is still used by *The Economist* and *The New Yorker* magazines, both of which spell cooperate "coöperate."

◆ The next time you worry that your kid is spending too much time with her imaginary friends, consider the Brontës. Well into their young adulthoods, the Brontës talked and wrote about two kingdoms they'd invented as children, Angria and Gondal. The Gothic, soap-operaesque storylines they invented in Angria and Gondal ended up informing both their poems and novels.

◆ Before they became famous, the Brontë sisters wrote poetry together. Using their gender-ambiguous pseudonyms, the Brontës published a book of poems in 1846. It sold exactly two copies.

The Buddha

Name-dropping: The Buddha (pronunciation: BOO-duh) (c. 563–483 BCE). Also known as Siddhartha Gautama and Gautama Buddha—the nirvana-achievin' founder of Buddhism who, contrary to what you might have heard, was neither Chinese nor obese.

When to Drop Your Knowledge: Buddhism is immensely helpful for late-night, really deep conversations. Like, have you ever thought about how everything—like, *everything*—is going to fall apart? You and me and the couch we're sitting on and the planet and everything? Well, the Buddha already thought of that, fortunately. And he did it without any intoxicants.

The Basics

Most of what we know about the Buddha isn't based on reliable histories but on legends, many of which weren't written down until centuries after the Buddha's life. But the story goes like this:

The Buddha was born a prince in an area that today straddles the border between India and Nepal. At the time, being a prince involved a life of carefree luxury (and, potentially, a Wilt Chamberlain–like promiscuity). But because a soothsayer told Siddhartha's mother that the baby would either grow up to be a great king or a great holy man, Siddhartha's father tried in vain to make him the former. In fact, he went so far as to shield the boy from any sort of religious

Four Noble Truths

The philosophy of the Buddha is often summed up in the following "Noble Truths":

1. "There is suffering." This one is fairly simple, and fairly obvious, too, and if you disagree we will come to your house and punch you in the face to prove you wrong.
2. The cause of suffering is desire. "Desire" here is not so much a reference to romantic desire as to one's general attachment to people, places, and things.
3. The way out of suffering is to eliminate desire.
4. The Eightfold Path is the way out of suffering. If you're wondering what the Eightfold Path is, well— then we've got a sidebar just for you.

education and exposure to human suffering.

When he was 29, however, Siddhartha started traveling outside the palace and encountered "the four sights": a crippled man, a diseased man, a rotting corpse, and finally a wandering ascetic, who roamed the hills of India much like the hippies once roamed the Haight. Siddhartha quickly became every parent's nightmare: He ditched his money, his parents, his wife, and his palace to spend his life searching for a way to overcome the inevitability of human suffering.

After a couple years of nearly starving himself to death as an ascetic, the Buddha sat down beneath a tree (called the Bodhi tree) and asserted that he wouldn't move a muscle until he found enlightenment. He found it, and from then on, Gautama came to be known as a "Buddha," or "Awakened One."

Initially preaching to just five people, the Buddha's disciples soon multiplied. Further, his teachings of impermanence and karma, along with the "Four Noble Truths" and the "Eightfold

Eightfold Path

1. The Right Perspective
2. The Right Thinking
3. The Right Speech (i.e., no lying)
4. The Right Action (i.e., no stealing, no killing, no intoxicants, and no sex if you're a monk)
5. The Right Livelihood (i.e., not being an investment banker. We kid. Sort of.)
6. The Right Effort
7. The Right Mindfulness
8. The Right Concentration

Path," became the foundation point for a philosophy and religious tradition that would, by the first century CE, be a driving force in the lives of people from India to China.

THE LOW-FAT PATH

The Buddha is often portrayed as being a bit—how to put this politely—fat. But was he? Probably not. The Buddha competed throughout his life in wrestling and archery, and he spent much of his time hiking great distances. Depictions of a fat Buddha are often not of Gautama at all, but of another Buddha named Hotei. An eccentric, pudgy, and happy monk, Hotei is known as the Laughing Buddha and is a common subject of Buddhist artwork.

Conversation Starters

◆ Before kabbalah, Buddhism was all the rage among Western celebrities. Fads pass, but a few have stayed loyal to the faith, including Richard Gere, Tina Turner (who has credited Buddhism for helping her to ditch Ike), and the Beastie Boys's MCA.

◆ Most Buddhists do not consider Siddhartha Gautama to have been either the first or the last Buddha. Since enlightenment is available to everyone (even if you are, say, a grasshopper), there have been many Buddhas throughout history. Those who achieve enlightenment but forgo nirvana, choosing to remain in the cycle of death and rebirth, are known as bodhisattvas—and these, too, are numerous and widely revered by Buddhists.

◆ In 2004, a Japanese candy manufacturer sought to register a trademark for a popular candy it produced called "Snot from the Nose of the Great Buddha." A group of priests stopped the company from getting the trademark for its gooey, sugary snack, but it remains on sale—complete with a wrapper depicting the Buddha beatifically picking his Buddha nose.

◆ From the Interreligious Dialogue Files: The Buddha, who lived well before Jesus, was once a Catholic saint. St. Josaphat, as he was known, was the son of an Indian king whose father tried to keep him from going religious. When it became clear to scholars, however, that Josaphat was, you know, the Buddha dressed in a saint suit, he was quietly taken off the list of saints.

Catherine the Great

Name-dropping: Catherine the Great (pronunciation: Just sound it out) (1729–1796). Russian Empress of German descent who did not—we repeat, *did not*—die during a botched attempt to have sex with a horse.

When to Drop Your Knowledge: First and foremost, whenever anyone tells that horrifying story about the horse. (More on that and the true circumstances of her death in a moment.) Why is it, anyway, that kings get to have wild, bacchanalian parties on a daily basis and no one ever raises a peep, but a woman has a little fun here and there, and all of a sudden she's in a romantic relationship with a horse? So, yeah. Whenever gender relationships come up.

The Basics

Catherine the Great started out pretty unlucky—well, as unlucky as German princesses can get. When she was 14, she was shipped off to Europe's hinterland to marry the heir to the throne of Russia, Karl Ulrich. That seems like a pretty good deal, maybe, until you consider that Karl was crazy, impotent, an alcoholic, and had a fanatical fascination with the emperor of Prussia, Russia's sworn enemy. After Karl assumed the throne in 1762, it quickly became obvious that he would be, like, the Worst Emperor Ever, and so a group amassed a small army and marched upon his castle. Terrified, Karl fled, and so just six months after Karl's coronation, Catherine—

When "My Kingdom for a Horse" Starts Sounding Dirty

Somehow, the rumor survives. Soon after Catherine's death, someone—probably her enemies in the Russian aristocracy—started floating the story that Catherine died of being crushed after attempting to have sex with a horse. Russian aristocrats may have started it, and high school boys have been spreading it ever since. But it's just not true. Although Catherine did take many lovers and had a secret room built in her palace that she filled with raunchy paintings and sculptures, Catherine the Great did not die anywhere near a horse. But the true story is nearly as embarrassing: Catherine the Great, empress of Russia, had a stroke while on the toilet, and died a few days later.

well-read, intelligent, and friendly with Enlightenment stalwarts like Voltaire and Diderot—was installed in his place. Her husband was assassinated by Catherine's supporters eight days later.

Although Catherine agreed intellectually with Enlightenment principles—most notably that the serfs ought to be freed from their functional slavery at the hands of landowners—she found it impractical to make such reforms, mostly because she relied on the support of landowners. But over the next 34 years, she did bring Russia further into the fold of Europe by modernizing her court, streamlining government bureaucracy, and building more than 100 new towns and cities. Although she was of German ancestry, Catherine embraced Russian culture wholeheartedly and served as a kind of PR representative for a nation that had always been considered backward by the rest of Europe.

Over the next 34 years, Catherine the Great would add 200,000 square miles to the Russian Empire. And she added over

200,000 lovers to her personal list of conquests. (We kid!) Although Catherine had many lovers, she was less promiscuous than the vast majority of male monarchs. And although her marriage was miserable, she found happiness in her relationship with Grigory Potempkin, an adviser who oversaw the annexation of the Crimea and advised her on countless construction projects.

In the end, Catherine paid more lip service than actual attention to Enlightenment ideals. And while the improvements she brought to Russia may not have been felt by the serfs (who constituted 95 percent of the population), the sheer force of her charisma and her determined intelligence improved Russia's image throughout the world.

THE GREATS, IN APPROXIMATE ORDER OF GREATNESS

Peter the Great (1672–1725): Probably Russia's greatest statesman. Also he was six-foot-seven! Sure, he wasn't great for the serfs—but then again, no one was. ★★★★★

Alexander the Great (356–323 BCE): Conquered half the known world and did it all before dying at 33. If he pulled those stunts now, he would be called a war criminal. Still, pretty great for his time. ★★★★

Catherine the Great (1729–1796): She could have been greater if she'd had the courage to stand up to the landowners, but if she'd done that, she'd probably have died violently and young. ★★★

Frederick the Great (1712–1786): Sure, he tried to be a genuinely enlightened monarch, but he also had a pathological fear of bathing. ★★

Pompey the Great (106–48 BCE): Friend to, and then enemy of, Julius Caesar. But if he was so great, how come he never became Caesar himself? ★

Conversation Starters

◆ The world-famous State Hermitage (which in Russian is pronounced err-mee-TAJJ) Museum began as Catherine's personal collection of art. She was generally a friend of the arts, although like a lot of Russian leaders, she couldn't help but send a dissident writer to Siberia now and again. Most famously, she exiled Alexander Radishchev to Siberia after he published a book highlighting the miserable lives of the serfs.

◆ Also like a lot of Russian leaders, Catherine just couldn't stomach the existence of Poland. Her forces invaded Poland in 1792, and eliminated it from the map (temporarily) by 1795, dividing it among her kingdom, Austria, and Prussia.

◆ Catherine was said to strongly dislike her son, who later became Emperor Paul I, but it's possible that this story—like the one about the horse—was created by her enemies in the aristocracy. Still, Paul seems to have believed Catherine hated him. As a young man, the perennially paranoid Paul accused his mom of mixing shards of glass into his food in an attempt to kill him.

# Charlemagne

Name-dropping: Charlemagne (pronunciation: SHAR-luh-main) (c. 742–814 CE). For 43 years, he was King of the Franks (the Franks being the forefathers of both the French and the Germans). You might think that having the same forefathers might keep France and Germany from getting into a gigantic war every few decades. But, hey. Cain and Abel. Union blue and rebel gray.

When to Drop Your Knowledge: During drunken poker games, whenever elephants come up, and—most significantly—when you get stuck talking to someone who is absolutely, positively fascinated by genealogy.

The Basics

Charlemagne means "Charles the Great" in French, and—indeed. He became king of a recently unified France in 771, when he was in his 20s, whereupon he immediately decided to invade and conquer Italy. Then he annexed Bavaria (for the beer, presumably), took over Hungary, and conquered parts of Spain. Before he was 40 years old, Charlemagne had unified most of European Christendom. And that was only the beginning.

Charlemagne's real gift was for infrastructure. He divided his kingdom into 350 well-run counties, rebuilt schools in France, and encouraged the growth of church music. He even experimented with a kind of pre-Republic in an annual, open-

Question: Who's Your Great[38] Granddaddy?

Answer: Charlemagne, if you're of European ancestry. We made a solemn vow not to do any difficult math during the writing of this book, so just take our word when we say that you have two parents, four grandparents, eight great-grandparents, and about a trillion great[38] grandparents (there's a lot of doubling, due to extremely distant incest). Ergo, everyone of European ancestry living today can count Charlemagne (and, incidentally, also the prophet Muhammad) as an ancestor. In fact, research indicates that every human being alive is probably a descendant of Queen Nefertiti and Confucius. One study claims that the chance Charlemagne *isn't* a European's great[38] granddad is about 1 in $10^{15,000}$. (By comparison, there are about 10^{80} atoms in the entire universe, so we're talking a very, very slim chance.)

air meeting with landowners during which he'd outline his plan for the coming year and then listen to their suggestions. (He didn't always take these suggestions, and he sometimes killed the landowners he disagreed with, but—baby steps!) However, Charlemagne wasn't in the pocket of the landlords, and he fought, with mixed results, against the growth of the serf system.

Charlemagne's chief passion, aside from war, was education. Like most nobles of his day, he received minimal academic instruction in his childhood, but he made his palace a kind of early university. The school's hardest-working student was Charlemagne himself, but unfortunately Charles the Great was a poor student. For instance, he never really learned how to, um, write. But he tried hard, studying rhetoric, astronomy, and Latin.

Cowboy of Hearts

Beginning in the mid-1400s, French playing card designers associated each king in a deck of cards with an actual, real-life king. In fact, even today the cards are associated with the royal links the French gave them.

- King of Spades—King David
- King of Clubs—Alexander the Great
- King of Hearts—Charlemagne
- King of Diamonds—Julius Caesar

In the coming Dark Ages, Europe would cease to be a center of the cultural world, but Europe flowered under Charlemagne as never before. And although he was an absolutely ruthless tyrant who would today doubtlessly be called a war criminal, he is the rare "Great" who earned the name.

POUND FOR POUND

Charlemagne introduced much of the world to the *livre*, known in English as the pound—both the monetary unit and the weight. In a world where princes often printed their own special currencies, Charlemagne applied his standards throughout his kingdom, and the English adopted them to ease trade. In time, Britain passed them to America. We Americans still measure in pounds; but all of Charlemagne's empire, and indeed nearly every other nation in the world, uses kilograms.

Conversation Starters

◆ Many contemporary accounts of Charlemagne record that he was, well, a bit of a girly man. Apparently, he spoke in an unusually high voice.

◆ Although Charlemagne is often remembered for his Christian piety due to his passion for sacred music and converting the masses, there was one commandment he just couldn't seem to follow: the one about killing. In just one day, for instance, he oversaw the beheading of 4,000 Saxons.

◆ According to legend, Charlemagne used to impress guests by throwing his tablecloth into the fire and then pulling it out unburnt. (These were simpler times, when people were impressed by Amazing Unburnable Tablecloths.) Those who believe the story is true provide a simple enough explanation: Charlemagne's tablecloth was likely made of asbestos.

◆ Somewhere around the beginning of the ninth century, Islamic caliph Harun al-Rashid gave Charlemagne an elephant. The elephant (whose name is lost to history) was sort of the Columbus of his species. He is believed to have been the first ever to venture into Northern Europe.

Miles Davis

Name-dropping: Miles Davis (pronunciation: You can handle this one) (1926–1991). Trumpeter whose hugely influential playing and composing puts him near the top of the list of important 20th-century musicians.

When to Drop Your Knowledge: Whatever sub-genre of jazz your cocktail party hosts happen to use for a party, there's a reasonably good chance that Miles Davis invented it, refined it, or redefined it—so Davis is sure to be a hit topic. Also, if your hosts happen to be heroin addicts, Davis serves as an excellent cautionary tale.

The Basics

Miles Davis was the rare serious musician whose work succeeded both critically and commercially. He stood at the forefront of most major jazz movements over the last 60 years of jazz, and he got rich doing it. (Miles liked to say, "I got five Ferraris to support!")

The son of a dentist, Davis started seriously playing the trumpet when he was 13. By the time he graduated from high school, he'd played with the likes of Dizzy Gillespie and Charlie Parker. In fact, he even got a full ride to Juilliard, but upon arriving in New York City, he decided to ditch school in favor of playing with Parker's quintet. Those recordings from the mid-1940s proved to be seminal achievements in

Best-Seller

Kind of Blue is the best-selling jazz record of all time. It has sold more than three million copies, and 40 years after its 1959 release, it was still selling 5,000 copies a week. (Incidentally, one would have to sell 5,000 albums a week for more than 47 years to match the sales of the Backstreet Boys's 1997 self-titled effort.)

Miles Davis always resented the white establishment, particularly after a 1959 beating at the hands of New York police officers. So this oft-told story rings true: In 1987, Miles attended a reception to honor Ray Charles and was seated next to a scion of Washington society. When she asked him what he'd done to get invited to the reception, he responded, "I've changed music four or five times. What have you done of any importance other than being white?"

bebop, the fast-tempo and heavily improvisational music for which Parker is best remembered.

Then Miles decided to follow in a storied tradition of jazz musicians and get himself addicted to heroin. For five years, it seemed that Miles's talent might go to waste, but he eventually returned to his hometown of East St. Louis and kicked heroin with the help of his dad the dentist (who, we're imagining, just threatened to drill his teeth sans Novocain if Miles kept shooting up).

In 1959, Miles released his masterpiece album, *Kind of Blue*. It made him both famous and rich. Davis called together his new band on almost no notice, gave them brief instructions, and sat down to play. The album was recorded in two days. All the songs but one were recorded in one take. Often called *the* definitive jazz album, *Kind of Blue* was revolutionary: It used modes rather than chord progressions, ushered in the era of "cool jazz," and—perhaps best of all—its emphasis on melody made it approachable for jazz neophytes.

By the early 1970s, Miles progressed to fusion jazz—using electric instruments and funk beats in the studio—producing the indisputable classic *Bitches Brew,* which marks the only time in this entire book that we get to use a curse word.

By the mid-1970s, his addictions to cocaine and alcohol (and heroin again) led to a physical and emotional breakdown. He dropped out of the jazz scene, got halfway sober, and returned to the public eye in 1981, but he was never quite the same.

THE ORIGINAL PIMP

Miles often dressed flamboyantly, particularly in the 1970s, when America seemed to believe that only polyester could save us from the threat of Communism. Between the flamboyant dress, the fast cars, and his many affairs, Miles has often been cited as an early example of living the pimping lifestyle without actually having to, you know, pimp. Except, he did, you know, pimp. According to the *New York Times,* Miles briefly worked as a pimp during his early heroin-addicted days in New York.

Conversation Starters

◆ In between winning 26 Grammys, writing music (including the theme for *Sanford and Son*), founding *Vibe* magazine, and be-friending everyone from Michael Jackson to Bono, Quincy Jones apparently finds an hour each day to share with Miles. He once commented, "[*Kind of Blue*] will always be my music, man. I play *Kind of Blue* every day—it's my orange juice."

◆ Miles once said, "I'll play it first and tell you what it is later," and that's more or less the approach he took to recording. He'd often call in band members on no notice, give them no time to rehearse, talk briefly about what he wanted to happen, and then start playing. Although this annoyed some of his band members (notably John Coltrane, whose playing Miles found long-winded), others found it exhilarating.

◆ In the Jazz Cat Imitating Spider-Man category: Davis's former road manager Chris Murphy claimed in a tell-all book that Davis once decided to scale the face of his apartment building because he had no key and was convinced that his girlfriend was in the apartment engaging in shenanigans with "a dozen white guys."

Dead Sea Scrolls

Name-dropping: Dead Sea Scrolls (pronunciation: obvious) (found beginning in 1947). Ancient scrolls containing most of the Hebrew Bible, a treasure map, and some excellent recipes for plum wine.

Essenes (pronunciation: EH-seens): A religious community of Jews living around the time of Jesus who probably penned a majority of the scrolls.

When to Drop Your Knowledge: When you're discussing *Ulysses* (see p. 164), for starters, since the scrolls contain even *less* punctuation than *Ulysses'* final chapter. But your knowledge of the Dead Sea Scrolls should also sufficiently impress armchair scholars of religious history.

The Basics

Often referred to as the greatest manuscript discovery of modern times (although we're still waiting for a bunch of Salinger novels to show up when the guy finally dies), the Dead Sea Scrolls were discovered along the northwest shore of the Dead Sea in 11 separate caves. (If you're driving from Jerusalem, head east until you get to Jericho and then hang a left.) Dating from sometime between the third century BCE and first century CE, the "scrolls" consist of 850 documents (not all of which were recovered in scroll form) written in Hebrew, Aramaic, and Greek.

Oddly enough, the scrolls weren't discovered by hardwork-

Alas, Poor Shapira

In 1883, an antiquities dealer in Jerusalem named M. W. Shapira decided to sell an ancient manuscript of the Book of Deuteronomy that he believed to be extremely valuable. But when he sent the manuscript to biblical scholars, they all agreed it was a forgery. Humiliated, Shapira committed suicide in 1884. The following year, the manuscript sold at auction (for much less than Shapira hoped to get for it), and promptly disappeared. But comparisons of the Dead Sea Scrolls to descriptions in stories of Shapira's manuscript have led scholars to believe that Shapira's Deuteronomy was quite probably authentic—and thus worth untold millions. Which just goes to show you: Never, ever kill yourself.

ing archaeologists but by a shepherd. In 1947, a boy named Muhammad edh-Dhib threw a stone into a cave in hopes of chasing out a goat he thought might have ambled into it. The stone shattered pottery, and when Muhammad entered the cave to investigate, he found the first scrolls. By 1956, all the extant scrolls had been recovered.

Most scholars believe the scrolls were written by a Jewish group known as the Essenes, who were driven out of Jerusalem because their apocalyptic worldview clashed with that of the Jewish leadership. The Essenes believed in a sort of *Star Wars* world: There was good, and there was evil, and there was not a lot of gray. The good (the "children of light") would soon conquer the evil (the "children of darkness." George Lucas came up with better names, at least). The group who wrote the scrolls seems to have been fixated on a messiah figure possibly living among them who's constantly referred to as the "Teacher of Righteousness."

Because the scrolls were written right around the time of Jesus, they have importance to scholars of both Christianity and Judaism. Jewish scholars have used them to learn more about the emergence of Rabbinic Judaism in the last centuries BCE, while Christian scholars have learned more about the apocalyptic religious movements in and around Palestine during Jesus' life. If nothing else, the scrolls reveal the diversity within Judaism at the time they were written, and help us to understand the Judaic world in the years before the destruction of the second Temple by the Romans in 70 CE.

THE SCROLL YOU WISHED YOU FOUND

Our personal favorite scroll is the so-called Copper Scroll, which is actually written on copper and contains a veritable treasure map of secret tombs containing silver, gold, and spices. Um, *Goonies 2*, anyone? We're picturing an aging Corey Feldman teaming with, say, Dakota Fanning, to seek out gold in them thar Holy Hills.

Conversation Starters

◆ Initially, many of the Dead Sea Scrolls didn't look like scrolls, but like a jigsaw puzzle. Scholars pieced together over 100,000 fragments of papyrus—a particularly impressive accomplishment when considering that most of the pieces were missing.

◆ Among the texts in the scrolls are some Thanksgiving psalms, a couple rocking hymns, and a divinely dictated battle plan. They also contain psalms attributed to King David and a host of sacred writings not found in the Hebrew Bible.

◆ Other than paragraph indentations the scrolls have no punctuation absolutely none which as you can imagine makes for difficult reading

☿ W. E. B. Du Bois

Name-dropping: W. E. B. Du Bois (pronunciation: due-BOYZ—don't feel bad if you couldn't pronounce his name; it was so common a problem that Du Bois sent a letter to a newspaper explaining how to pronounce it correctly) (1868–1963): Cofounder of the National Association for the Advancement of Colored People and author of the classic *The Souls of Black Folk*.

When to Drop Your Knowledge: Whether you're chatting with an exchange student from Ghana about her homeland, a board member from the NAACP about the organization's history, or a ditzy sociology major you're about to make out with on account of your breadth of knowledge and wisdom, Du Bois can carry you through. He's versatile like that.

The Basics

In 1895, Du Bois became the first African American to get a PhD from Harvard. His degree was in history, but his passion was sociology, and he was soon famous in academic circles for his brilliant sociological studies, particularly the book *The Philadelphia Negro* (1899).

Du Bois might have stayed a scholar—he had a plum gig teaching at Atlanta University and was widely respected—but his life in the South led him to believe that writing sociological treatises for a narrow audience wasn't going to end Jim Crow. In 1903, he published *The Souls of Black Folk*. Perhaps no book

Communism: It Wasn't Just for Idiots and Meanies

The attraction of Communism, which offered revolutionary change and equality for the working class, was profound indeed. Many African American intellectuals in the first half of the 20th century expressed Communist sympathies, including Richard Wright, Paul Robeson, and Langston Hughes. And though you don't read about it in schoolbooks, another American icon who stood for the rights of the disenfranchised, Helen Keller, was a member of the Socialist Party in the U.S. Not *technically* Communist, but close.

since Harriet Beecher Stowe's *Uncle Tom's Cabin* so ignited passion and conflict about the place of African Americans in society. Unlike his contemporary Booker T. Washington, Du Bois believed that voting and other rights were more important to African Americans than working within the segregation system. *The Souls of Black Folk* is the rare book that's considered a classic by English professors, sociologists, and political scientists alike.

Du Bois was also the first writer to apprehend the "double-consciousness" of African Americans—the idea that being black and American led to "two souls, two thoughts, two unreconciled strivings." The book established him as a rival to Booker T. Washington for the title of Most Important Black Leader in America.

In 1909, Du Bois cofounded the NAACP, and he edited its flagship magazine, *The Crisis*, for 25 years. But he eventually fell out with NAACP leadership. In his later years, Du Bois came to embrace the radical egalitarianism of Communism. He visited Communist China, called Stalin "a great man," and generally irked the FBI, which eventually indicted him on a trumped-up charge that he'd become a "foreign agent." The case never came to trial, and Du Bois eventually solved his legal troubles and his personal "double-consciousness" problem at the age of 92—by ceasing to be an American. Invited to live in Ghana by its president, Du Bois—who'd always favored pan-African unity—left the U.S. and renounced his citizenship. Although he died a Ghanaian, no American in the first half of the 20th century did more to influence the civil rights movement of the second half.

A NOVEL APPROACH

Du Bois is remembered almost exclusively for his nonfiction writing, but he was a novelist as well—albeit not a very good one. If you think *Moby Dick* features a lot of information about whales and whaling, check out how Du Bois nitpicks cotton to death in *The Quest of the Silver Fleece*.

Conversation Starters

◆ W. E. B. Du Bois was a frat boy. But what a frat! During his days at Fisk University, Du Bois was one of the most prominent early members of the historically black fraternity Alpha Phi Alpha. Among his brothers: Jesse Owens, Duke Ellington, Paul Robeson, and Dr. Martin Luther King Jr.

◆ Like a lot of great men, Du Bois had a weakness when it came to infidelity. He lived with his wife, Nina, for 53 years, but Du Bois himself acknowledged, "It was not an absolutely ideal union." For one thing, it was nonideal in the sense that Du Bois had periodic affairs, including some that scholars refer to as "parallel marriages."

◆ Although the National Association for the Advancement of Colored People clearly stated its mission right in its title, Du Bois was—get this—the only African American on the NAACP's first board of directors.

◆ Du Bois died in Ghana just one day before the epochal March on Washington began. Martin Luther King Jr. eulogized Du Bois the following morning at the start of the march, a sort of preparation for his brilliant "I Have a Dream" speech.

The Dutch East India Company

Name-dropping: Dutch East India Company (pronunciation: like it sounds) or Vereenigde Oostindische Compagnie (pronunciation: um, like it sounds—in Dutch). Massive commercial enterprise of the 17th century.

When to Drop Your Knowledge: Every cocktail party features someone who enjoys talking about their business, even though their business is unfathomably boring. Before you find yourself nodding off to a discussion about the profit margin of coffee filters, interrupt them with a story from the Dutch East India Company, which did business in a day when doing business meant war, bravery, torture, immense wealth, and—most of all—nutmeg.

The Basics

Spices were to 16th-century Europe what Air Jordans were to 1990s Harlem: Even though people had lived quite happily for centuries without them, they were suddenly worth killing for.

Established in 1602, the Dutch East India Company (also known by its Dutch abbreviation, VOC) obtained a monopoly over Dutch colonial activities in Asia. And thanks to its dominance on spices like nutmeg and pepper, the VOC soon became the largest company in the world. At its height in the

The Name Game

The end of colonialism was an unmitigated disaster for cartographers. Dozens of places changed names; borders changed; new countries formed and old ones were swallowed up. (The Democratic Republic of the Congo holds the record, with five name changes in the past century.) Most every place ruled by the Dutch East India Company has since rechristened itself, as you can see:

Persia	→ Iran
Bengal	→ Bangladesh (and parts of western India)
Siam	→ Thailand
Ceylon	→ Sri Lanka
Formosa	→ Taiwan → Republic of China
China	→ Okay, still China. But you get the point.

late 17th century, the VOC had a private army of 10,000 soldiers, 150 merchant ships, and 50,000 employees. It was also the first company to issue shares of itself in stock, the first to issue bonds, and the only company in all of history to have controlled dozens of colonies throughout the world. (Take that, Wal-Mart!)

The key to the Dutch East India Company's success? Why, exploitation and murder, of course. The most successful head of the VOC made the CEOs of Enron and WorldCom look like patsies. Jan Pieterszoon Coen, who ruled the VOC from 1617 to his death in 1629, massacred most every grown man in the Pacific Bandalese archipelago to cement his control over the islands. In fact, within 15 years of the VOC's arrival, the islands' populations had been reduced from 15,000 to 600. Later leaders of the VOC were hardly more compassionate—by the end of the 17th century, the punishment for stealing or unauthorized growing of nutmeg or clove was execution.

All that tyranny took a toll on the bottom line, however. Manning a sizable army, complete with 100 warships, isn't cheap, and despite its best efforts, the Dutch East India Company couldn't keep a monopoly on spices. French and British entrepreneurs stole seedlings and planted them on their own colonial lands, and the competition drove down the price of spices. By the mid-18th century, the VOC was kept afloat primarily by its network of textile mills. Then, in 1799, the first great company went bankrupt. The VOC, which once billed itself as the "Grandest Society of Merchants in the Universe," ceased to exist. By cornering the market on spices, it proved that a luxury product could lead to huge profits. By issuing stock, it ushered in modern publicly traded corporations. And the Dutch East India Company did it the old-fashioned way: It pulled itself up by its bootstraps, secured the support of a powerful government, and relentlessly killed and tyrannized all those who got in its way.

The British East India Company and the VOC were hated rivals, and they frequently battled for control of the spice trade. In 1619, the Brits and Dutch signed a treaty allowing the British one-third of the spice industry and the Dutch two-thirds. A good deal for the Dutch, but not good enough. In 1623, the Dutch attacked a British East India factory in the Pacific. The Brits who died immediately were the lucky ones: The survivors were tortured by having their arms and legs systematically blown off by small gunpowder bombs. *Then* they were killed.

Conversation Starters

◆ Even though the sophisticated and worldly palates of today realize that nutmeg tastes like a mix between cayenne pepper and grandma's basement, Renaissance Europe was nuts for the stuff. The Dutch East India Company wanted nutmeg so much, in fact, that they acquired the nutmeg-laden island of Pulo Run, one of the Banda Islands, from the British in exchange for the colony of New Amsterdam, which the British renamed New York.

◆ Much has been made of the dangers of sailing to the Far East, but working for the VOC wasn't as risky as you might think: In the 16th and 17th century, only 4 percent of the ships that traveled to the Far East were lost. (By comparison, being an American president is significantly more dangerous than being a Dutch East India Company ship: About 9 percent of American presidents have been assassinated.)

◆ In one of the first examples of outsourcing, the VOC closed its shipyard in 1649, realizing it would be more profitable to hire others' ships than to build its own. In 1669, the dividend payment on VOC shares was 40 percent of the stock price. (In 2003, Microsoft's dividend was .03 percent.)

Galileo Galilei

Name-dropping: Galileo Galilei (pronunciation: ga-li-LAY-oh gal-li-LAY-ee) (1564–1642). Italian scientist and mathematician who made several extraordinarily important discoveries. Almost all of which, incidentally, proved that Aristotle—for all his fame and brilliance and everything—was sort of an idiot.

When to Drop Your Knowledge: It's late. The party is winding down. You've been chatting for the past three hours with a person to whom you're deeply attracted. You've regaled them with the wit of Samuel Johnson and the wisdom of the Qur'an. And now, it's time to take that person outside and stare up at the heavens together. And when that special person you met two hours ago looks deep into your eyes, inches a little closer to you, and his/her lips begin to part, it's time to make your move: Start talking about what happened to Galileo when he pointed out the sky didn't revolve around us.

The Basics

Galileo's first significant contribution to science traditionally is said to have occurred atop the Leaning Tower of Pisa, when he supposedly dropped bodies (as in objects, not dead people) and proved that the speed of a falling object is not proportional to its weight, as Aristotle claimed. Before Galileo, everyone believed Aristotle, because—hey—he was Aristotle.

Galileo and the Scientific Method

So how come no one ever dropped a couple rocks from a cliff to check and make sure that Aristotle was right about the behavior of falling objects? Because until that point no one had invented the Scientific Method (aka the cornerstone of all modern science), wherein a hypothesis is developed and tested. Galileo's credit for developing the Method, however, must be shared with Sir Francis "Don't Call Me Sausage" Bacon. Between the two of them, they revolutionized the manner in which people approached the questions of the heavens.

(In reality, Galileo's experiment probably involved rolling objects down an incline, not dropping them off a tower, but that's not as good a story.) Galileo further contradicted Aristotle by proving that projectiles take parabolic trajectories (you'd think someone would have noticed this with all the catapulting that went on in the Middle Ages, but no).

Galileo was a pious and unassuming fellow who never sought to court controversy. But for some reason, he kept discovering things that disproved conventional wisdom. Fortunately, debunking Aristotelian physics never got anybody excommunicated from the Catholic Church. Unfortunately, Galileo started meddling in astronomy. At first, it seemed his observations made him rich and secured his fame. Having discovered four moons around Jupiter, he smartly named them after the ruling Medici family, who responded in kind by getting him a sweet gig in his native Tuscany.

But he soon noticed that Venus revolved around the Sun, which flew in the face not only of Aristotle's beliefs, but also those of the Catholic Church. After keeping quiet on the issue

Heliocentrism

Galileo was neither the first nor the only scientist to believe in a heliocentric universe. The idea was first put forth by Nicolaus Copernicus, who didn't publish his work for decades and then had the good sense to die just after it finally saw the light of day, before anyone could get mad at him.

for nearly a decade, Galileo received permission from the pope to write a book on the topic. The resulting work, succinctly titled *Dialogue Concerning the Two Chief World Systems, Ptolemaic and Copernican*, in which a character named Salviati explains that the earth clearly revolves around the Sun, and a guy aptly named Simplicio is constantly ridiculed for his irrational belief in an earth-centric universe.

Summoned to Rome for an Inquisition, Galileo eventually apologized (legend has it that at the end of his apology, he mumbled, "And yet—it moves,") and was sentenced to life in prison. The "prison" proved to be a small, comfortable villa near Florence, where he continued to work, albeit with his heart broken by the Church to which he remained ever faithful.

IT'S A MATH, MATH, MATH, MATH WORLD

Although Galileo didn't devote much time to the study of pure mathematics, he did make a discovery that baffled mathematicians for 250 years: He proved that there are as many perfect squares (1, 4, 9, 16, 25, etc.) as there are whole numbers (1, 2, 3, 4, 5, etc.), even though the vast majority of whole numbers are not perfect squares. Known as "Galileo's Paradox of the Infinite," this caused headaches for abstract mathematicians until the early 20th century, when Georg Cantor invented set theory, which has been causing headaches for Calculus II students ever since.

Conversation Starters

◆ In 1609, Galileo learned that a telescope had been invented by Hans Lippershey in the Netherlands. Unable to procure one from the inventor, he jerry-rigged his own contraption using three lenses he purchased at an eyeglass store. Then, with a little trial and error, Galileo eventually learned the fine art of grinding lenses—producing the most powerful telescope in the world. Aside from allowing him to chart the universe, his high-powered spyglass also proved definitively that the moon's surface was not smooth, as scientists had previously thought, nor was it made of Swiss cheese, as scientists had secretly hoped.

◆ Like a lot of successful people, Galileo was a college dropout. He briefly attended the University of Pisa, but had to leave because he couldn't afford tuition. Just a couple years later, however, he ended up returning to college—this time as a professor.

◆ Galileo was also a prodigious inventor: Besides his work with the telescope, he invented the first compound microscope, a complicated air-and-water-based thermometer, and the first driver for a pendulum clock. (Among the inventions he sketched but never got around to making are a comb that doubled as an eating utensil, an automated tomato picker, and a ballpoint pen.)

Gods of Olympus: the Ladies

Name-dropping: Olympus (pronunciation: oh-LIM-pus). The mountain that the 12 baddest gods and goddesses in Greek mythology called home. Occasionally, Zeus would call the whole crew together for a meeting on Olympus ("Good to see you again, Dionysus," Zeus would say. And Dionysus would respond, "Hey, Zeus. Remember that time I was born out of your thigh? That was so weird"). But mostly Olympus was occupied by the 12 men and women profiled here. In an attempt to remedy the patriarchal oppression inherent to the Greek pantheon, we'll start with the goddesses.

When to Drop Your Knowledge: If you see your Special Someone flirting with Someone Else at a party, you'll need Hera. Also, the next time you spill red wine on someone's ivory white carpet, you can pass it off as an offering to Hestia.

The Basics

APHRODITE

Doubling as the goddess of romance and beauty, the stunning Aphrodite was married to Hephaestus—the hardest-working (yet, not the most attractive) god in the business:. Unfortunately for him, she cheated frequently with mortals and gods alike (not surprising, since the word *aphrodisiac* does derive from her name).

ARTEMIS

A proud virgin, Artemis was the goddess of the hunt and chastity. Flanked by her companions (who were also all virgins), she roamed the forests hunting for lions and panthers. In short, she was a bit of a tomboy. But despite her reputation for healing and kindness, it was Artemis who was believed to bring and spread leprosy and rabies.

ATHENA

The goddess of war strategy and wisdom, Athena was wildly popular with the ancient Greeks, so much so that Greece's capital is named for her. When Poseidon and Athena were vying for the city's affections, Poseidon threw his trident into a hillside and a spring emerged from the hill. But the water was salty (that Poseidon was always screwing things up). Athena's gift, an olive tree, was less spectacular, but it provided food *and* wood *and* oil (the original Giving Tree). So, it's no wonder the Athenians swore their allegiance to her.

DEMETER

Ancient Greece's goddess of earth, Demeter was worshipped by rural Greeks for her association with the harvest. In spite of the fact that she is often portrayed wearing ears of corn as a crown, Demeter was considered quite beautiful. Unfortunately, she got the least attractive-sounding name of all the Greek goddesses: It doesn't exactly roll off the tongue in English, and in Greek it means "barley mother."

HERA

Queen of the gods and Zeus's wife, Hera might have been happy if only Zeus had been loyal to her. But Zeus's relentless infidelity infuriated her, and because she couldn't really take it out on the Big Z, she mostly punished his illegitimate children (like Dionysus, whose foster parents were driven insane by Hera). Unfortunately, she was depicted as petty and unforgiving because she didn't acquiesce to Zeus's cheating—a clear sign that male chauvinism extended to the heavens.

HESTIA

The goddess of home life, Hestia was the only *chill* deity on all Mount Olympus. While everyone else was out raining fire, famine, and earthquakes from the heavens, Hestia chose to spend most of her time on earth doing nice things for the mortals.

Conversation Starters

◆ Just as Eazy-E poured malt liquor on the ground to honor his fallen comrades, ancient Greeks often poured wine on the ground to honor Hestia, the only goddess who was ever consistently nice to them.

◆ Not only did Hera manage to perennially regain her virginity, some ancient sources also claimed she could get herself pregnant without assistance from hubby Zeus. How'd she manage that neat trick? Depending on the source, Hera achieved self-impregnation either 1. by slapping her hand on the ground or 2. by munching on lettuce.

◆ Although America generally picks either presidents or Native Americans for our coinage, the "heads" side of the heaviest coin ever produced by the U.S. Mint depicted none other than the Greek goddess of war, Athena.

◆ And you thought that scene in *Alien* was upsetting: According to some ancient sources, Aphrodite's birth was a bit unusual. She spontaneously arose from the severed genitals of Uranus. (Cronos, a young Titan, cut them off in a fight, whereupon they fell into the sea.) Nineteenth-century painter William-Adolphe Bouguereau managed to make this birth story beautiful in his famous painting *Birth of Venus* (Aphrodite's Roman name), which depicts a naked and—we'll just say it—really hot Aphrodite rising from the sea.

Gods of Olympus: the Fellas

Name-dropping: God (like it sounds). Today mostly known for his compassion, justice, infinite power, and knowledge. But back in the day, the gods of Olympus were as petty, jealous, and lame as people—only more powerful. In continuing our introduction to the Olympian deities, we turn now to the boys.

When to Drop Your Knowledge: Nothing ends a miserable conversation with a drunk who wants to take you home quite like "I wonder if I should ask Poseidon or Zeus to smite you. Zeus's lightning would be faster, but Poseidon's trident might be more fun to watch."

The Basics

ZEUS

King of the gods, Zeus looked a little like Santa Claus, but without the cheery disposition. Wielding his trademark thunderbolt, Zeus ruled over Olympus *and* earth, justly resolving disputes and putting people and gods in their proper place. But don't mistake his greatness for goodness: Zeus *constantly* cheated on his wife, Hera (who was also his sister), had innumerable illegitimate children, and would transform himself into almost anything (bull, swan, whatever) to bed a fair maiden.

DIONYSUS

He didn't live on Olympus, but the god of alcohol is, almost by definition, the god of cocktail parties—so no cheat sheet would be complete without him. Dionysus mostly used his powers for the forces of good. For example, when a Greek deity misbehaved, Dionysus would show up, the offender would get so drunk s/he'd pass out, and then things would be made right.

APOLLO

The hottest of the male Olympians, Apollo was also an archer the likes of which hasn't been seen outside of Middle Earth elfdom. Combine his good looks with the fact that he was the god of poetry and music, and it's no surprise that Apollo did well with the ladies.

ARES

The god of war, Ares was loved by Aphrodite but hated by most everyone else (in *The Iliad*, Zeus says to him, "To me you are the most hateful of all gods who hold Olympus," which really hurts coming from your dad). Ares was said not to care who won or lost a battle so long as the fight was bloody.

POSEIDON

King of the sea and earthquakes, Poseidon was one of the gods least friendly to mortals. He was also associated with horses, so it's no wonder Greek sailors often drowned a horse before voyages to avoid his wrath.

HEPHAESTUS

The God of fire and blacksmiths, Hephaestus is also known as "the Greek god we always forget exists." It was Hephaestus who, with the help of some cylcops, forged Zeus's thunderbolts

Greek to Roman

As previously noted, it's best to use the Greek names for gods if you want to seem intellectually up-to-date. But if nothing else, understanding the Roman names helps you to realize just how many planet namings the Greeks got screwed out of.

GREEK	ROMAN
Zeus	→ Jupiter
Apollo	→ Apollo
Ares	→ Mars
Poseidon	→ Neptune
Hephaestus	→ Vulcan
Hermes	→ Mercury

and his scepter. He also made arrows for Eros, who would later be called Cupid.

HERMES

The messenger of the Olympian gods, Hermes had the unenviable job of escorting mortals to the underworld when their time came. He wore a winged helmet, sort of like Viking fans, and was also associated with bringing dreams to mortals during sleep.

FROM HUNCHBACK TO DREAMBOAT

Hephaestus was the ugliest deity on Olympus, and was usually portrayed as having a lame leg. So the ancient Greeks would no doubt be surprised to learn that their little lame Hephaestus, known to the Romans as Vulcan, is today the subject of the world's largest cast-iron sculpture. Built in 1904, Birmingham, Alabama's Vulcan stands 56 feet tall, weighs 120,000 pounds, and shows the god's bare (and decidedly *not* lame) derrière. The bare buns caused a scandal when the state of Alabama tried to place the statue in downtown Birmingham. For 30 years Vulcan gathered dust at the Alabama State Fairgrounds. But today he stands tall and proud and very muscular atop Birmingham's Red Mountain.

Conversation Starters

◆ With his trident and beard, Poseidon bears a bit of a resemblance to Christian portrayals of Satan. Coincidence? Probably not entirely. Early Christians often associated Roman gods (like Poseidon, or as he was known in Rome, Neptune) with the evils of paganism—and many scholars argue that Satan's trident, if nothing else, has its roots in Neptune.

◆ Poseidon may not have been Satanic, but he *was* a bit odd. One of his main interests was trying to have sex with his sister, Demeter, who, needless to say, didn't swing that way. In fact, when Demeter turned herself into a mare to resist his advances, the clever (and extraordinarily perverted) Poseidon transformed into a stallion and proceeded to mate with her. Boy, they sure don't make gods like they used to.

◆ It was prophesied that Zeus's father, Cronus, would be overthrown by one of his children. So, like any quick-thinking god, Cronus swallowed each of his kids as they were born. Only Zeus, the youngest of the six, was saved from Cronus's mouth, and when he became a young man, he convinced his dad—honestly—to puke up Zeus's five brothers and sisters. The siblings—Demeter, Hestia, Hera, Hades, and Poseidon—were all fixtures in the Greek pantheon, but they each deferred to their little brother and savior (and husband, in Hera's case).

Han Dynasty

Name-dropping: Han (pronunciation: like Solo) dynasty (pronunciation: like the TV show) (206 BCE–220 CE): A model for all future Chinese dynasties, the Han changed the history of China. If you have to pick a dynasty to know, this is the one.

When to Use Your Knowledge: When you see some ancient-looking Chinese art. You've got a fair chance of being right if you say, "Wasn't this painted/sculpted/drawn/thought up during the Han dynasty?"

The Basics

The founder of the Han dynasty was a minor official named Liu Pang, who raised an army and overthrew the corrupt and generally pretty horrible Ch'in dynasty in 206 BCE. Liu Pang renamed himself Kao Tsu (Chinese leaders, like Russian cities and Diddy, frequently renamed themselves) and began to revitalize Chinese government and society.

For one thing, Kao Tsu brought Confucianism to the fore of Chinese government. With its emphasis on moderation, reverence for authority, and scholarship, Confucianism was a good match for Kao Tsu's style of governance. While promotion within the government was based on merit and Kao Tsu encouraged artistic and intellectual achievement, he ruled with an iron fist and expected all Chinese citizens to submit to his will.

Fu

The predominant form of creative writing during the Han dynasty, *fu* was a combination of poetry and prose that got its beginning in Qu Yuan's classic poem "On Encountering Sorrow." With an unrestrictive rhyme pattern and extremely long lines, *fu* was less lyrical than previous Chinese poetry, so writers could go on and on with exposition. In the writing business, this is called "telling instead of showing" and is generally frowned upon. (Think of the achingly bad poems written by Ryan to Trista on *The Bachelorette*.) Indeed, although a few *fu* writers are well esteemed today, most were hacks who knew that writing poetry improved your chances of getting promoted in the government bureaucracy. Imagine that: a world in which writing poetry (even bad poetry) can *help* get you promoted.

The Han dynasty became known for its artistic and cultural achievements. They created a Music Bureau, for instance, that cataloged all known musical instruments and styles of playing. The Han dynasty also saw great advancements in technology: Perhaps because they kept such extensive records, the Han eventually abandoned bamboo as a writing surface and invented paper. And they invented the first working seismograph, which could detect earthquakes from hundreds of miles away.

The Han dynasty also saw the emergence of the "Great Silk Road," which is a bit of a misnomer, because 1) it was not made of silk, and 2) there was not an actual road involved. But it was definitely great. The Han pioneered the route from China through central Asia (i.e., the 'Stans—Uzbekistan, Kazakhstan, etc.) to the Mediterannean. Using this route, the Chinese exported elaborate silk weavings and spices as far west as the

The First Toilet

The Han dynasty saw the invention of countless tools we've come to take for granted (like paper, as previously noted, and also the collapsible umbrella). But it seems it might also have given us that greatest of conveniences: the toilet. In 2000, archaeologists in China discovered a toilet, complete with a stone seat and running water. The toilet was found not in a Han dynasty house but in a tomb!

Roman Empire. Thus, the Han dynasty sent China down a path of exporting goods to the West that would eventually culminate in the greatest cultural achievement of *our* time: Wal-Mart.

The Han dynasty lasted more than 400 years— longer than any other in Chinese history. It was toppled, however, by a peasant rebellion fueled by the Taoist beliefs in equal rights. After decentralization, the last Han emperor was finally overthrown in 220 CE. Even today, however, China views the Han dynasty as the apex of Imperial Chinese history.

BIG RELIGION IN LITTLE CHINA

The peace and prosperity that Confucianism helped bring to China during the Han dynasty also led to the arrival of Confucianism's greatest rival: Buddhism. In the middle of the Han dynasty, with trade routes open to the west and south, Buddhism traveled freely from India to China, where it would take hold to such a degree that even today, it is easy to forget that Buddhism originally came from India.

Conversation Starters

◆ Despite embracing Confucianism, which emphasizes scholastic study, Liu Pang himself was a coarse peasant who didn't think much of book learnin'. He once peed into the hat of a court scholar (who fortunately was not, at the time, wearing the hat) to show his lack of respect for education.

◆ Hearing all the names of the many Chinese dynasties, one can't help but wonder how China managed to fit so many *dynasties* into just a few thousand years. Don't dynasties, by their very nature, require at least a few generations? Not so much, as it turns out. Immediately preceding the Han, for instance, the Ch'in "dynasty" barely even hit puberty before petering out. It lasted all of 15 years.

◆ The Han dynasty is so central to China's identity that the Chinese word for "Chinese person" literally translated to "a man of Han."

◆ When Liu Pang was fighting for power after the fall of the Ch'in dynasty, his main rival was named Xiang Yu. Xiang Yu captured Liu Pang's father and then sent a bold message to Liu Pang: "Surrender or I will boil your venerable sire alive!" Liu Pang responded: "Send me a cup of the soup." You can take your Keyzer Sozes and your Corleones and your Tupacs. For sheer *cojones*, we'll take Liu. His father, incidentally, ended up surviving—not that Liu seemed to care much.

The Hundred Years' War

Name-dropping: The Hundred Years' War (pronunciation: duh) (1337–1453). A sporadic fight between (who else?) England and France that, despite its name, managed to go on for 116 years. Featuring a Black Prince, a guy nicknamed "the Bold," a guy nicknamed "the Good," and a whole bunch of siege-ing, the Hundred Years' War is sort of like J.R.R. Tolkien's *Lord of the Rings* trilogy—only longer.

When to Drop Your Knowledge: In discussions of war. Also, whenever anyone accuses the French of being inherently wimpy or slow to take decisive action, you can point out that this wasn't always the case. They were once very brave and quick to take bad actions.

The Basics

Between 1337 and 1453, France and England engaged in a series of battles over what amounted to a disagreement about some land. In 1328, Edward III of England, who was also duke over part of southwestern France, decided that France should probably go ahead and make him king. A French assembly disagreed, making Philip VI king of France. When Philip made a move to take Edward's land in southwestern France, Edward got mad and started a war. (And who can blame him? The south of France is lovely.)

Extra Credit:
WHAT IS IT GOOD FOR?

Sure, it lasted a long time and killed a lot of people, but did the Hundred Years' War accomplish anything worthwhile? Absolutely. Whereas France had often been a nation divided up by independent aristocrats, the Hundred Years' War instilled in her a sense of national identity that has lasted—for better or worse—to the present day. And it increased nationalist feelings in Britain, too. No longer did British monarchs see expansion into Europe as the only way to become a great king. British leaders began to look inward—which initially led to civil war but eventually to the fostering of a British identity that included the Scots and Welsh. Of course, no one really learned their lesson. Within a few centuries, after all, Britain would colonize half the world.

In those days, wars were fairly boring affairs. Lengthy sieges were followed by the occasional battle for a town, so it took a number of years before anyone even knew who was winning. Eventually, it became clear the British were faring better than the French. Edward's son, known as the Black Prince, even managed to capture the French king (who was by now John II) in 1356.

By 1421, the British seemed to be in excellent shape. They controlled much of France, including Paris. The French king, Charles VI, suffered from what was probably schizophrenia, while the British king, Henry V, was a superb leader. But then Henry V and Charles VI both died, and British fortunes changed. Suddenly, the new French king, Charles VII, if nothing else, wasn't schizophrenic, while the new British king, Henry VI, was eight months old. Not yet being potty-trained, young Henry couldn't exactly lead his men into battle. France began to rise anew.

Then Joan of Arc came along and, with her volunteer forces, liberated the city of Orléans from the Brits in 1429. Joan got burned at the stake for her efforts, but she changed the hearts of several key players, who decided to start fighting for the French. By 1453, the British were defeated, and France was free.

WELCOME TO THE GUN SHOW

The Hundred Years' War saw the widespread introduction of firearms and artillery to the European battlefield. In fact, the war's last battle, that of Castillion, is said to be the first European battle in which cannons proved the deciding factor. The British were mowed down by French cannons during an ill-advised attack on the well-fortified French lines. The British dead included their commander, John Talbot, whose horse was killed by cannon fire. Trapped beneath his ride, Talbot died the old-fashioned way: He met with the unfriendly end of a Frenchman's battle-ax.

Conversation Starters

◆ The Battle of Castillion proved to be the last of the Hundred Years' War. But it might have flared up again had not British king Henry VI, who inherited the throne at the age of eight months, gone bonkers. Henry likely suffered from bipolar disorder starting in 1453, scholars say. But at the time, there was neither effective treatment nor accurate diagnosis: As far as his court was concerned, Henry just became stark raving mad for months at a time, and was completely unable to process anything that went on around him.

◆ Edward III and Philippa had twelve children—seven sons and five daughters—and their many, many direct descendants would end up duking it out for the right to lead England in a protracted civil war that came to be known as the War of the Roses. Some historians have speculated that if he'd chosen to have fewer kids (you'd think all that warmongering would have kept him busy) and therefore fewer descendants, the War of the Roses might never have occurred.

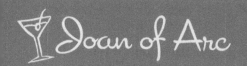
Joan of Arc

- **Name-dropping:** Joan of Arc (like "Joan of Arcadia" without the "-adia") (c. 1412–1431). French girl who, in spite of being a female in a sexist world, and in spite of being thought insane by many who encountered her, and in spite of being a little kid from a peasant family, basically turned the tide of the Hundred Years' War (which a total of 10 French and British kings had failed to do).
- **When to Drop Your Knowledge:** Joan of Arc can be useful when people start talking about the question of whether women should be allowed in combat. But she'll also come in handy if you're ever at a cocktail party and begin to hear invisible voices. Don't freak out. Stay calm. You could be going crazy, or you could be just a couple years away from tremendous success and renown. Followed by, um, a horrible execution.

The Basics

In a time when French peasants had few rights, and French peasant women had even fewer, a teenage Joan of Arc somehow managed to meet the king of France and convince him to let her lead the French royal army into battle.

When Joan was born, the internal strife within France caused the nation to periodically forget that they were engaged in the Hundred Years' War with England. In all that chaos, it's no wonder the English king, Henry V, began

Extra Credit:
SECRET SIGNS

Joan of Arc never allowed her troops to fight on Sunday. In fact, she might have further routed the English at the Battle of Orléans, except that the clever Brits started their retreat on a Sunday. And *she's* the heretic?

One of the enduring mysteries of Joan's story is why, exactly, Charles VII chose to trust her. He dressed in disguise on the day she visited the palace, and Joan immediately picked him out of the crowd—but Charles never really trusted Joan until she shared with him a "secret sign." Some historians believe that Joan told Charles she was aware of his worry that he might have been born illegitimately. Joan then assured him his birth was legitimate, which made Charles so happy that he sent her off to war. After her arrest, though, he did nothing to save her.

grabbing huge chunks of French territory for himself. Joan was by all accounts a quiet, pious child. Then, around the age of 13, she started hearing voices. The Archangel Michael, St. Catherine, and St. Margaret began conversing with Joan, telling her that she needed to drive the English out of France. The rational Joan listened to these voices for about three years before finally approaching a commander at the local fort and asking him to take her to King Charles, because the Archangel Michael had told her that she could defeat the English.

There's no record of the commander's exact response to Joan's request, but we imagine it was something along the lines of *"Tu es très crazy."* But a few months later, she returned to the same commander, and this time—improbably—he believed her. He gave her an escort of six soldiers, who apparently dressed her in male clothes and brought her through enemy territory to the king.

Amazingly, the king soon grew to trust young Joan. He gave her permission to take a small band of soldiers to the city of Orléans, where her orders were to try to end the English siege of the city. In the first week of May, 1429, Joan won a series of battles against the English, who soon abandoned their attack on Orléans. Suddenly, no one in France thought Joan was crazy. By June, the French were routing the English: At the Battle of Patay (not Pâté), 2,200 English soldiers died compared to just 20 Frenchmen. Joan desperately wanted to move on and take Paris, but Charles was slow to act. When the assault on Paris finally did begin, Joan suffered an arrow to the breast, and the attack failed.

On May 23, 1430, Joan was captured by a captain named John of Luxembourg, who handed her over to the British in exchange for what would today amount to several hundred thousand dollars. Accused of heresy in a show trial, Joan was convicted on the grounds that her voices could not possibly come from God, since clearly God wanted the English to control France. She was burned at the stake on May 30, 1431, but remained a faithful Christian to the last. Among her final words were "Hold the cross high so that I may see it through the flames."

Conversation Starters

◆ Throughout his later years, Samuel Clemens did not consider *The Adventures of Huckleberry Finn* or even *Life on the Mississippi* to be his greatest literary accomplishments. Instead, he believed that his fictionalized history *Personal Recollections of Joan of Arc* would be remembered as his best book. Twain was mistaken, though. Overly serious and written in a maudlin style, the book is rarely read, even by Twain fans.

◆ Widely admired for its theological sophistication, the canceled CBS show *Joan of Arcadia* featured a young woman named Joan who talks to God and takes action to make the world a better place. Its replacement, *The Ghost Whisperer*, starring Jennifer Love Hewitt, is about a girl who talks to ghosts. Why the change? According to CBS chief Les Moonves, "I think talking to ghosts may skew younger than talking to God."

◆ Throughout her military career and even during her imprisonment by the English, Joan preferred wearing men's clothes.

◆ Joan has long been the patron saint of France, but it seems that she might have also become the unofficial patron saint of artsy indie-rock bands suffering from perennial depression. She's been mentioned in songs by Silverfish, Catatonia, and Garbage, among others. Our favorite Joan of Arc namedropping occurs in "Bigmouth Strikes Again," by the Smiths: "And now I know how Joan of Arc felt, as the flames rose to her Roman nose and her Walkman started to melt."

Samuel Johnson

Name-dropping: Samuel Johnson (pronunciation: Oh. Come on) (1709–1784). Critic, poet, playwright, biographer, lexicographer, college dropout, and all-around swell guy most famous for standardizing the English language.

When to Drop Your Knowledge: Knowing a few of Johnson's quips will go a long way toward making you look sophisticated at any cocktail party. He'll also be helpful when you find yourself talking to one of those people who begins to mangle the English language after one cosmopolitan. When you start hearing "libary" and "schoolastic," you can just hand them Sam Johnson's *Dictionary of the English Language* and walk away.

The Basics

Samuel Johnson lived the American Dream in Britain—although he never thought much of America. (He once commented, "I am willing to love all mankind, except an American.") The son of a bookseller, Johnson appeared headed for a life of mediocrity. At 28, he was a failed schoolteacher when he headed to London with nary a penny in his pocket. That is, of course, until he found work writing for magazines. Pretty soon, his wit and keen literary and political criticism were sweeping the nation.

Johnson's most important work, *A Dictionary of the English*

The Language According to Dr. Johnson

Johnson's dictionary is generally quite serious and straightforward, making his whimsical entries all the more fun. A sampling:

Lexicographer: A writer of dictionaries; a harmless drudge . . .

Oats: A grain, which in England is generally given to horses, but in Scotland appears to support the people.

Tory: One who adheres to the ancient constitution of the state, and the apostolical hierarchy of the Church of England, opposed to a Whig.

Whig: The name of a faction.

(Johnson, needless to say, was a Tory.)

Language, was published in 1755. Although dictionaries had been compiled before, he was the first to include examples of the defined word from the works of great writers, which helped to establish a canon of English literature. As dictionaries go, Johnson's makes for a surprisingly fun read (see sidebar) and, being the work of a single man, represents a Herculean accomplishment.

While composing the dictionary, he also wrote a biweekly column for the magazine *The Rambler*, which is widely considered to be his best prose work. Still, poor Sammy never had much money until 1762, when the government began issuing him an annual pension. Although his dictionary defined *pension* by saying, "In England it is generally understood to mean pay given to a state hireling for treason to his country," Johnson accepted the money. He was never poor again, and spent the remainder of his long life as the toast of British literary society.

COCKTAIL PARTY CHEAT SHEETS

The Quotable Johnson

On remarrying: "[It is] the triumph of hope over experience."

On its alternative: "Marriage has many pains, but celibacy has no pleasures."

On writing: "No man but a blockhead ever wrote, except for money."

On sailing: "Being in a ship is being in a jail, with the chance of being drowned."

On cucumbers: "A cucumber should be well sliced, dressed with pepper and vinegar, and then thrown out."

Although he is often referred to simply as Dr. Johnson, the "Dr." came from an honorary degree at Oxford conferred upon him later in life. Johnson was really a college dropout: Unable to pay tuition, he left Oxford after one year.

Johnson might never have achieved the lasting fame he so deserved had it not been for his young protégé James Boswell, whose brilliant and heartbreaking *Life of Johnson* ranks as one of the greatest biographies ever written, and ensured that the talented Dr. Johnson would have fans for centuries. No magazine writer before or since ever achieved such notoriety (trust us—we are ourselves a magazine writer, who toils in obscurity behind the Royal We).

Conversation Starters

◆ In defense of Ashton Kutcher: When he was just 25, Johnson married a 46-year-old widow named Elizabeth Porter, who in spite of having a perfectly good name insisted on going by "Tetty." Very shortly after Tetty died in 1752, Johnson took up with a woman with an even *funnier* name, Hill Boothby.

◆ Johnson liked to say that he was born "almost dead." Bouts with lymphatic tuberculosis and other ailments left his face heavily scarred from childhood. He was also blind in one eye, partially deaf, and suffered throughout his life from a severe facial tic, leading most modern experts to conclude he suffered from Tourette's syndrome.

◆ Johnson was famous for his insults. Here, for instance, is an early example of the great literary genre the lawyer joke: When asked his opinion of a certain individual, Johnson said, "I do not care to speak ill of any man behind his back, but I believe the gentleman is an attorney."

◆ Johnson had a reputation for being a slow writer, but his satirical novel *Rasselas* was written in two weeks—he needed to pay for his mom's funeral.

Kama Sutra

Name-dropping: Kama Sutra (pronunciation: KA-muh SUE-truh) (Written sometime between 30 and 400 CE). Literally meaning "aphorisms on love" or "treatise on pleasure," the *Kama Sutra* is an ancient Indian text most famous for containing 64—*sixty-four!*—"arts." And by "arts," the *Kama Sutra* means "positions."

  Vatsyayana: Purportedly the author of the *Kama Sutra*, although no one knows anything about who he was or when he lived or whether he was a single person or a bunch of people or whether he even existed. All we know is that *if* he existed, he got a lot of play.

When to Drop Your Knowledge: Everywhere and always. Like George Clinton songs and homemade guacamole, the *Kama Sutra* is bound to be a hit at any party.

The Basics

The *Kama Sutra* is most famous for the second of its five sections, "On Sexual Union." It's in this section that the reader is introduced to the 40 kinds of kissing, varieties of orgasm, and the aforementioned 64 sexual positions. Also, it's here that Vatsyayana argues that there are eight positions possible within each of the broader ways of having sex. (We'd include some pictures here, but the publisher said we couldn't.)

  But the *Kama Sutra* is not some guide to a Bacchanalian lifestyle. Vatsyayana believed that frivolous sex was sinful.

The Talented Mr. Burton

Richard Burton (the one who lived from 1821–1890, not the one who twice wed Elizabeth Taylor) spoke dozens of languages, traveled the globe in search of adventure, was considered the greatest swordsman of his century, and managed to translate both the *Kama Sutra* and *The Arabian Nights*. But in his own day, he was most famous for being the first Christian known to have taken part in the Islamic Hajj. Non-Muslims are not allowed into the holy city of Mecca during the annual Islamic pilgrimage. But in 1853, Burton disguised himself as a Muslim—he studied Islam for months in advance and even went so far as to have himself circumcised (just in case anyone checked). After all, Islam, like Judaism, requires circumcision of males. The travel book that resulted, *Pilgrimage to El-Medinah and Mecca*, secured Burton's renown—and we're happy to defer to anyone who loves adventure enough to endure adult circumcision.

Further, he believed in the importance of treating people well. For that reason, the dirty-dirty only comprises about 20 percent of the total text. Parts of the book, for instance, remind people how to live well. But most of it is a sort of ancient Indian *Men Are from Mars, Women Are from Venus*. In exploring how to acquire a wife (or how to seduce another person's wife), Vatsyayana discusses the differences between men and women and how each gender experiences pleasure.

The *Kama Sutra* was helping Indians have fuller sex lives for at least a millennium before the British explorer, swordsman, raconteur, and all-around dreamboat Sir Richard Burton decided to translate the text. (Let's just say that Burton had found it helpful.) Burton's classic 1883 translation is still widely read today, and even though it was censored in England, it found

Extra Credit:

KAMA

"Kama," is not a kind of chameleon, although, due to Boy George's poor pronunciation, we believed otherwise until quite recently. "Kama" is, in fact, the Hindu god of love. And just like Cupid, Kama is often portrayed shooting love-producing arrows—which just goes to show that there's a real cross-cultural appreciation for the relationship between getting stabbed with an arrow and falling head over heels.

a rabid audience throughout Europe and—eventually—in America. Today, the *Kama Sutra* is perhaps unfairly synonymous with sexual experimentation. It also has served as an important source for scholars seeking to understand ancient India.

WHAT'S A VATSYAYANA?

Very little is known for certain about the life of Vatsyayana. For instance, scholars have only gotten within five centuries of nailing down the time when he lived (between the first and sixth centuries CE). One of the most pervasive rumors about Vatsyayana is that he spent a great deal of time with prostitutes in order to research his *Sutra*.

Conversation Starters

◆ When Richard Burton first visted India, he was assigned by the British government to investigate homosexual brothels. His inflammatory report, which showed that many British soldiers and officers made frequent visits to such brothels, led to him being fired from the Army. By the time he translated the *Kama Sutra* in 1889, he'd learned his lesson: Victorian Brits were prudish. Instead of using English words to describe genitalia, he used the Sanskrit words *lingam* and *yoni*. The latter caught on as a slang word in English for a woman's genitalia.

◆ Now and again, the *Kama Sutra* offers some questionable advice. Say, for instance, you want a virgin to marry you. You might buy the virgin an engagement ring, or even start referring to her by her first name instead of always calling her "the virgin." Or you could follow the advice of the *Kama Sutra* and throw a mixture of vajnasunhi powder and monkey dung over her head.

◆ Among the studies that Vatsyayana asserts are vital to be a full and complete lover: architecture, gemology, metallurgy, and magic. (This points to the disconcerting conclusion that the folks from *Extreme Makeover: Home Edition* might be really great lovers.) Knowledge of these fields, of course, made one a proper husband back then—and only a proper husband could be a proper lover.

◆ And for those of you who might be really bad people: An entire chapter of the *Kama Sutra* is devoted to how best to seduce other men's wives.

John Maynard Keynes

Name-dropping: John (pronunciation: like the Baptist) Maynard (pronunciation: like a May nerd) Keynes (pronunciation: like *canes*) (1883–1946). Arguably the greatest economist of the 20th century, Keynes is so famous that he has an *-ian* word. His, Keynesian, means using fiscal spending programs to stimulate business and increase employment.

When to Drop Your Knowledge: Economists love sitting around and talking about Keynes, because he was the rarest of economists—he never lacked for company in bed. But knowledge of Keynes will also serve you well when amateurs discuss everything from the Fed's interest rate to unemployment levels.

The Basics

Son of the economist John Neville Keynes, John Maynard quickly eclipsed his father's fame. In 1919, he published *The Economic Consequences of the Peace*, which correctly predicted that the enormous burdens on postwar Germany would lead it to economic ruin and fierce nationalism. Sadly, his fellow Brits didn't listen until the Nazis started dropping bombs on them, at which point the world collectively realized that this John Maynard Keynes fellow was either psychic or a *really* good economist.

The Even Keel

Keynes's ideas have been used by governments and fiscal policymakers to stabilize economies, keeping them from growing too fast or too slowly. Broadly, when the economy is growing quickly, Keynes suggested, governments ought to raise taxes and decrease spending in order to rein in inflation. When the economy is in recession, he recommended, governments should lower taxes and increase spending to kick-start the economy. This concept of balanced growth would have prevented the rampant inflation of 1930s' Germany and softened the blow of the Great Depression elsewhere. And it continues to work well today—the Federal Reserve in America still raises and lowers interest rates to balance inflation with growth.

In 1936, Keynes's most influential work was published. Titled *The General Theory of Employment, Interest, and Money*, it argued that recessions don't fix themselves—which had never occurred to anyone, even though they were all in the depths of the Great Depression. Keynes argued that the solution to recession was a proactive effort by governments to stimulate the world economy. It was on the strength of this book that Keynes became known as the father of macroeconomics, which is admittedly akin to being the father of a famously boring child, but still better than most of us will ever do. Keynes went on to participate in the conference that led to the creation of the International Monetary Fund and the World Bank, two institutions that would help to shape and stabilize the postwar global economy.

In addition to his hard work forever changing the history of economic policy, Keynes was something of a party animal. In his younger years, he had a number of romantic relationships with men—including a seven-year relationship with

British painter Duncan Grant. Partly because of his standing in society (Keynes was a baron) and partly because homophobia had begun to lessen (a few decades before, the discovery of Oscar Wilde's homosexuality led to his arrest and imprisonment), Keynes's bisexuality was never that much of an issue. He married a prominent Russian ballerina named Lydia Lopokova in 1917, and although they were unable to have children, their marriage was by most accounts a happy one.

Although the fundamentals of Keynesian economics remain influential, macroeconomics has changed since Keynes left the scene. Today, economists focus more on increasing gross domestic product than Keynes did, and his notion that the government should sponsor full employment is particularly unpopular. (Many macroeconomists think some unemployment is *good* for an economy, though try telling that to the people without jobs.) Still, Keynes's influence is felt widely: Every time a college kid falls asleep in a macroeconomics class, for instance, he has John Maynard Keynes to thank.

THE GENERAL THEORY OF BUSINESS

Some have speculated that part of the reason Keynes's *The General Theory of Employment, Interest, and Money* made such a splash upon its publication in 1936 was that it was *cheap*. In the Great Depression, scholars couldn't afford just any book, and at a price half that of most similar titles, *General Theory* was made accessible to a wider variety of politicians and economists.

Conversation Starters

◆ Keynes had a weakness for hack medicine. An oddball doctor (Keynes called him "the Ogre") sought to treat Keynes's generally poor health with bed rest and ice packs on the chest. Keynes died (while under the Ogre's care) in 1946 at the age of 62. His last words were, "I should have drunk more champagne." Sure, and covered your chest with fewer ice packs.

◆ Keynes was no stranger to contradiction. It's often said that during his life Keynes professed every possible opinion at least once. His explanation for the inconsistency was, like Keynes himself, equal parts disarming and charming: "When the facts change, my opinions change."

◆ Keynes ended up pretty rich, but not nearly as wealthy as Warren Buffett, the billionaire investment banking genius whose Berkshire Hathaway corporation has consistently beaten the stock market. Buffett has frequently cited Keynes as an inspiration for his investment strategies.

◆ An economics joke: Keynes and a friend from college took a trip to Africa in the 1920s. While there, the two had their shoes shined by some boys. Keynes gave his shoe-shiner a stingy tip, and when his friend suggested Keynes ought to give more, Keynes replied, "I will not be a party to debasing the currency." Yowza! What a zinger! Of course, the joke was probably less funny to the unlucky sap who'd just shined Keynes's shoes.

King Arthur

Name-dropping: King Arthur (pronunciation: you know) (fifth or sixth century, assuming he was real). A guy who may have lived during the sixth century in what is now Britain, or possibly never lived anywhere at any time. Regardless, his is the name that spawned a thousand fantasy novels.

When to Drop Your Knowledge: King Arthur can rescue you, with his trademark gallantry, from many a boring conversation. Whether you're chatting with a fan of Keira Knightly, creative anachronism, Monty Python, or young adult fantasy novels, knowledge of Arthurian legend is a must.

The Basics

If King Arthur existed, he was probably a Brit living in the late fifth and early sixth century CE who fought the Saxons. But aside from a few vague references to Arthur in first millennium stories, it's difficult to pin all that down. In truth, the historicity of Arthur doesn't matter all that much. His significance lies in the stories about him that were passed down to us, and *that* tale begins with Geoffrey of Monmouth.

In 1133, Geoffrey (who, like Geoffrey the Toys Я Us giraffe, has no last name) published *Historia Regum Britannie,* a bestseller (or the 12th century version of a bestseller, anyway) that tells the story of Arthur. Through his tale, the gallant king, with the help of some gallant knights and some

Other Round Tableans

Lancelot. The greatest knight of the Round Table, and Guinevere's lover.

Percival. The star of the quest for the Holy Grail, and the knight of the Round Table with the nerdiest name.

Galahad. The purest knight of the Round Table, he was taken up to heaven after finding the Grail.

Merlin. The Round Table's crazy wizard, who is the inspiration for most every fictional wizard since.

Guinevere. The Round Table was for Boys Only, but Guinevere—as queen consort and Lancelot's lover—casts a constant shadow on the boys' goings-on.

Despite its portrayal in *Indiana Jones and the Last Crusade,* those searching for the Holy Grail weren't looking for a bejeweled wineglass. They were after an ordinary-looking (if very old) shallow bowl, not unlike a kitten's water bowl, used by Christ at the Last Supper. (The word *grail* comes from the old Latin *gradalis,* meaning "a flat dish.")

distressed damsels, became *the* romantic hero for all England. Here's how it would go: Arthur gathers his knights (see sidebar) at the world-famous Round Table at Camelot (which would sometimes feature the wizard Merlin). They would set off on a series of crazy quests—most famously a search for the Holy Grail. After a series of hurdles, they achieve their goal.

And that, more or less, is the plot of most every happy-ending novel ever written. Those were not, however, the only endings. Many of the stories concluded with Arthur's death in the battle of Camlann, fought against his son, Mordred, or with an affair between Arthur's knight Lancelot and Queen Guinevere resulting in the downfall of Camelot. Those two endings represent the two prominent types of not-happy-ending stories—death and the loss of power. Such is the significance of Arthurian

Excaliburs

Arthur's sword Excalibur, which he famously pulled from a stone, is probably the most famous sword in all of history. But don't discount these:

The Man: Julius Caesar
The Sword: Yellow Death (Crocea Mors)
So called because: nobody who got struck by it lived to tell the tale.

The Men: Ancient English Kings
The sword: Curtana
So called because: of Irony, perhaps. Though "curtana" means the cutter, the Curtana itself was always blunt, emblematic of mercy.

The Man: Charlemagne
The Sword: Joyeuse
So called because: Apparently, using it made Charlemagne "merry," which explains his fondness for beheadings.

legend. Although stories of Arthur and Camelot were certainly not the first to use these plotting techniques, they were among the most influential and widely read.

Arthur and the residents of Camelot have proven to be a durable set of characters—they've been used everywhere from Tennyson's *Idylls of the King* to Twain's *A Connecticut Yankee in King Arthur's Court* to the Saturday morning cartoon *Gargoyles*. That's a résumé King Arthur can live with—assuming, of course, he ever lived.

Conversation Starters

◆ The film *Monty Python and the Holy Grail*, which is unquestionably the greatest film ever to emerge from the Arthurian legends, features at one point a picture of "God." "God" is actually 19th-century cricket player W. G. Grace, who was the Babe Ruth of cricket (Grace's career lasted 36 years). He also looked—there's no denying it—a lot like modern depictions of God, complete with the full, thick beard.

◆ A large percentage of the budget from *Holy Grail*, incidentally, came from donations given by members of rock bands Led Zeppelin and Pink Floyd.

◆ In 1522, British king Henry VIII (he of the many wives, some of whom were beheaded) ordered that his replica of Arthur's famous Round Table be painted with a likeness of King Arthur. Unfortunately, no actual image of Arthur was available, but this didn't dissuade the king. Never a modest chap, Henry decided that the image of Arthur in the painting should be modeled after, you guessed it, Henry VIII.

◆ Some sources assert that King Arthur, while he was really great and everything, might have had a slight problem with incest (which, in his defense, was pretty rampant back then). They claim that Mordred was the child of Arthur and his half-sister Morgause.

Vladimir Ilyich Lenin

Name-dropping: Vladimir Ilyich Lenin (VLAD-uh-meer EEL-itch LEN-in) (1870–1924): Russian Revolutionary whose Bolshevik Revolution would, many decades later, lead to the classic Nintendo game *Rush 'n Attack,* as well as several James Bond movies, the nuclear arms race, and Baby Boomers spending their childhood cowering beneath their school desks during nuclear preparedness drills. In short, he changed the world.

When to Drop Your Knowledge: When you're hanging around with communists or capitalists. Lenin is like a box of chocolates: You can pretty much find whatever you're looking for in his story.

The Basics

Born Vladimir Ulyanov, the man who would be Lenin came to hate the Russian monarchy early: When he was just 17, his older brother was hanged for conspiring to assassinate Czar Alexander III. Like a lot of people who would go on to do horrible things, Lenin became a lawyer, but rather than practice law he immediately became a full-time revolutionary.

From 1895 on, Lenin lived in periodic exile, always in trouble with the Czarist regime. But somehow he still managed to move up the ranks of the small socialist political party in Russia, until he eventually became the leader of the group known as the Bolsheviks in 1903. Like many a revolutionary, his first attempt at overthrowing the government, in April 1917, failed, mainly because the workers didn't rise up in quite the numbers he expected. The result: He ended up fleeing to Finland. But by October, the Bolsheviks began another offensive. Thanks to their cool, sloganny posters that now grace so many college dorm rooms, and also thanks to their guns, the Bolsheviks took Russia by storm. Not surprisingly, they proved to have a fair amount of popular support, and Lenin soon found himself in power—although the war between the Bolsheviks (or Reds) and Loyalists (or Whites) continued until 1920. It was the first successful Communist revolution, and Lenin's dictatorial style of Communism would become every bit as influential as Marx's writings.

Between the civil war and World War I, Russia was in bad shape by the time the shooting stopped. Lenin sought to turn things around with his New Economic Policy, which aimed to rebuild industry and improve agricultural techniques. (It did so, although a lot of peasants starved in the process. For presumably being on the side of the peasants, the Bolsheviks sure killed a lot of them.)

Lenin continued to be the leader of the Soviet Union until his death in 1924, but in reality, he didn't do much leading in the last few years of his life. After a debilitating stroke in 1922, he became an ineffectual leader—which, in part, gave noted jerkface Joseph Stalin the opportunity and time to assume control of the Soviet state.

A RIVER RUNS THROUGH IT

No one knows for sure when Vladimir Ulyanov picked the pseudonym Lenin. Maybe all the good nicknames (like "Stalin," which means "Man of Steel") were already taken. Some scholars, however, believe that "Lenin" was a subtle jab at fellow Communist Georgi Piekhanov, who'd chosen the pseudonym "Volgin," a reference to the Volga River. The Lena River is longer and flows in the opposite direction to the Volga—but hence "Lenin."

Conversation Starters

◆ Lenin asked that no memorials be created for him, so he might be a bit disappointed to learn that his embalmed body has been on display in Moscow's Red Square more or less continually since 1924. But how much of Lenin remains to be displayed is a question of open debate. In the past couple decades, Lenin's embalmed corpse has looked awfully waxy, and although the Soviet government won't comment, many believe that at least part of Lenin's body is fake. (The type of embalming most commonly used in the United States, incidentally, lasts only about a week.)

◆ One thing's for sure: Like the Scarecrow in *The Wizard of Oz*, the Lenin in Red Square doesn't have a brain. It was removed before his body was embalmed and sent to a German scientist in hopes that he could locate the brain cells responsible for genius. Either Lenin wasn't a genius or the brain is more complicated than the early Soviets believed, because the scientist didn't find much worth noting.

◆ Among Lenin's more unusual hobbies was sharpening pencils. As his brother Dmitry once noted, Lenin sharpened pencils with "a sort of special tenderness, so the letters came out like delicate threads." Sharpening pencils was apparently not just a childhood fascination; it continued into his Revolutionary days. Lenin also loved riding bicycles. Hey, even Communist revolutionaries need hobbies.

John Locke

The Basics

John Locke was a complicated figure about whom it is difficult to say anything with much authority. His belief in "government with the consent of the governed" and the inherent liberty of all people formed the cornerstone of democracy, particularly in the United States, and his philosophy and morality were hugely important in the Enlightenment and forever after. But paradoxically, he embraced slavery, and his philosophy at times reads like mere hedonism.

But before he was famous as the forefather to the American forefathers, Locke studied medicine. Although he was never licensed as a medical doctor (not that it meant much in

His Cheating Heart

Locke believed that the primary point of a marriage was to bear and raise children. Locke himself never married or had children, but he may have participated in some cheating. Locke fell for Damaris Cudworth (who, although you wouldn't know it to look at her name, was a woman), one of the first British women to publish philosophical writings. John and Damaris exchanged love poems, and later they lived together (with Damaris's then husband, Sir Francis Masham, and his eight children, oddly enough) for a number of years, leading to speculation that Locke might have cuckolded Mr. Masham.

17th-century Britain), his medical studies led him to take up residence with the (later) earl of Shaftesbury. Locke successfully treated the earl for a liver infection, and the earl was so grateful that he agreed to patronize Locke, which would now be an insult but back then meant "I will give you money and you don't have to do any work."

In the coming years, Locke would write two books that have been forced upon college students ever since. *An Essay Concerning Human Understanding*, written over a period of 18 years, is a philosophic treatise concerned in part with the differences between how we learn simple ideas (like "red") and how we learn abstract ones (like, for instance, "liberty").

Two Treatises on Civil Government, his most famous book, was concerned with that very liberty. It was here that Locke expressed his belief that all human beings—whether serf or king—were born with the right to life, liberty, and property. This wasn't the sort of thing that one ought to say when living under the rule of a king, so Locke didn't acknowledge his authorship of the treatises for many years. But it's a good thing that he did—his excellent reputation as the man who paved

In the Course of Human Events . . .

. . . it sometimes becomes necessary to plagiarize. Thomas Jefferson toed the line between inspiration and outright theft in the Declaration of Independence. Sure, there's nothing wrong with borrowing Locke's conceptions of liberty and freedom. But Jefferson's famous assertion that people have a natural right to "life, liberty, and the pursuit of happiness" comes perilously close to Locke's assertion that people have a natural right to "life, liberty, and property."

the way for the democratic revolutions in Europe and America is due entirely to that one short book.

THE PHILOSOPHICAL FRAT

Along with a small group of fellow Oxford students, John Locke formed the Experimental Philosophy Club, which sounds like a really dumb club. That is, until you consider that some of the other members included Robert "Father of Chemistry" Boyle, Christopher "Architect of St. Peter's Cathedral" Wren, and Robert "Inventor of the Modern Microscope" Hooke.

Conversation Starters

◆ Locke's theories on childhood, as outlined in *Some Thoughts Concerning Education,* might not fly with today's child labor laws. For instance, he expressed regret that poor children's labor "is generally lost to the public until they are 12 or 14 years old," and believed that kids from families on welfare ought to attend a sort of vocational school for toddlers, so as to be "from infancy inured to work."

◆ In the 1660s, Locke contributed to the text of the "Fundamental Constitutions" for the territories of the Carolinas in the New World. Although Locke professed to believe in the natural freedom of all people (well, men) and that enslavement created a "state of war," the Fundamental Constitutions of Carolina granted slave owners total ownership over their slaves. Like we said, he wasn't the most consistent of moral philosophers.

◆ Although his most famous books are short, college students everywhere complain that Locke had a tough time expressing a thought succinctly. Take this famous quote, for example: "I doubt not, but from self-evident Propositions, by necessary Consequences, as incontestable as those in Mathematics, the measures of right and wrong might be made out." Just come out and say it, Johnny: People can know right from wrong.

So perhaps it's no surprise that Locke's self-written epitaph on his tombstone runs 137 words.

Machiavelli

Name-dropping: Niccolò Machiavelli (NEEK-o-low mak-ee-a-VELL-ee) (1469–1527). Florentine writer and diplomat whose *The Prince* we were all supposed to read in high school but didn't, because while it is extremely short, it somehow also manages to be extremely boring.

When to Drop Your Knowledge: Every cocktail party has its evil dictator: the one who yells when speaking softly would suffice, monopolizes the resources by constantly hovering around the food and drink, and ruthlessly murders perfectly pleasant conversations with unfunny jokes. The Cocktail Party Dictator may believe his malevolent antics are justified by Machiavelli—but with your knowledge of the first great political philosopher, you'll be able to explain that Machiavelli wasn't nearly as evil as his totalitarian disciples.

The Basics

Born to a prominent family down on its luck, Niccolò Machiavelli was, in life, little more than a midlevel diplomat in Florence. Think of him as similar to the U.S. Ambassador to Fiji. Can't recall the name of the U.S. Ambassador to Fiji? That's our point.

And had Machiavelli kept his government job, he likely never would have become famous. His early writings, which had scintillating titles like "On the Way to Deal with the Rebel Subjects of the Valdichiana," were forgettable. But in 1512, the

The Quotable Machiavelli

On friendship: "You should keep your friends close, and your enemies closer."

On how not to have a happy marriage: "It is better to be feared than loved."

On the Second Amendment: "Before all else, be armed."

On acting rashly: "The wise man does at once what the fool does finally."

One Bad Marriage

Machiavelli was married for 25 years to Marietta Corsini. It rather goes without saying that he cheated on her frequently. (The ends of wanting to make out, after all, justify the means of breaking your marriage vows.) Marietta was a loving and devoted wife, but it seems Machiavelli never thought much of marriage: In one of his plays, a devil chooses to return to the fires of hell rather than spend time with his wife.

Medici family returned to power in Florence, and Machiavelli was fired. Accused of conspiring against the Medicis, he was briefly tortured and thrown into jail. Unable to find a job after his release, Machiavelli had time on his hands, so he wrote two works that would change the world: *Discourses on the First Ten Books of Titus Livius* and *The Prince*.

In the *Discourses*, Machiavelli asserted his belief in democracy as the best possible form of government. He did, however, endorse a kind of amorality—the *Discourses* mark the first appearance in political philosophy of the idea that the ends justify the means. He believed Florence was too weak and corrupt to support a republic. So in 1513 he wrote *The Prince*, his most famous and most controversial work, a kind of primer for would-be tyrants. What Italy needed, Machiavelli believed, was a "redeemer," a man who would

Machiavellian

One of the surest paths to immortality is to get a word named after you—but sometimes the price of fame is association with malevolence. Below, enjoy our guide to bad words and the bad people they're named for.

Machiavellian: Meaning "characterized by cunning and treachery." From the fellow in question.

Draconian: Meaning "extremely, unnecessarily harsh." From seventh-century Athenian politician Draco, whose codification of Athens's legal code was considered too severe.

Luddite: Meaning "one who stubbornly opposes techno-logical advancement." From Ned Ludd, a British work-man who supposedly destroyed weaving equip-ment around 1779.

Bowdlerize: Meaning "to censor or prudishly edit." From Thomas Bowdler, who, in keeping with the exces-sive prudishness of the times, published an expurgated version of Shakespeare in 1818.

rule with an iron fist, crush dissidents, build up the military, and rein in the malevolence in human nature. In short, you have to screw the people to save the people.

Machiavelli never achieved wide fame for his work during his life, but *The Prince* has been in print ever since—and more than a few modern dictators have used it as a blueprint, particularly in postcolonial Africa and South America. Because *The Prince* is so quotably blunt (see sidebar), Machiavelli has been a bit unfairly maligned. His contributions to philosophy and political theory are immense—he was the first person, for instance, to note the now trite maxim that history repeats itself. So really, a truly Machiavellian person isn't evil so much as relentlessly pessimistic and consistently unlucky—your basic philosophical Rodney Dangerfield.

Conversation Starters

◆ Some argue that "Old Nick," a slang term for the devil, derived from Machiavelli's first name, Niccolò, which would mean that we have Machiavelli to blame not only for despotism, but also for the Adam Sandler vehicle *Little Nicky*. Which is the greater crime? We'll leave that for you to decide.

◆ Although he courted the favor of several popes, Machiavelli didn't think much of Christianity, what with its emphasis on meekness, humility, and justice. But then, the popes of the time weren't such great Christians either. Leo X, who gave Machiavelli a job, spent the Vatican into bankruptcy and then tried to get out of it by selling get-out-of-hell-free cards called indulgences. The moral vacuity of the indulgences led, at least in part, to the Protestant Reformation that would irrevocably split the European Church.

◆ Besides being a revolutionary political philosopher, Machiavelli was also a published poet. It's hard to imagine a guy like Machiavelli writing good poems—fortunately, he didn't. His poetry is universally regarded as drivel.

◆ Tupac Shakur, the thinking man's gangster rapper, read from Machiavelli extensively during a stint in prison. Late in his career, Tupac began recording under the name Makaveli. Why the changed spelling? Well, maybe Tupac wanted to play on the gangster slang word "mack," which can mean flirting (to put it mildly) or a gun (Mac-10). But conspiracy theorists who believe Tupac's death was faked point to the fact that Makaveli is an anagram of "K, am Alive." Not the strongest evidence perhaps, but how's this: Since his (purported) death in 1996, seven (seven!) new Tupac albums have been released.

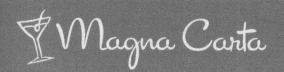
Magna Carta

Name-dropping: Magna Carta (MAG-nuh CAR-tuh—Latin for "Great Charter") (agreed to in 1215). Document granting certain liberties to the English people (by which we mean mostly "English landowning men") that, in retrospect, seems sort of like the first step toward democracy. At the time, however, it just seemed like a fun and easy way to avoid civil war.

When to Drop Your Knowledge: Like the Articles of the Confederation and the Big Mac Special Sauce, the Magna Carta is something we've all heard of but in the end don't know a lot about. So you're bound to impress people by dropping it into conversations about, for instance, the Big Mac Special Sauce. "I mean," you'll say, "I know more about King John's grudging ratification of the Magna Carta than I do about this special sauce."

The Basics

King John's acceptance of the Magna Carta in 1215 set a precedent (albeit one that wouldn't always be followed) for English monarchs: It established that monarchs were subject to earthly law. Future generations of Britons would use clauses from the Magna Carta to assert their right to a fair trial, and the U.S. Constitution would be inspired by it as well. (All this from a document that was basically plagiarized!)

In the year 1100, King Henry I issued a "Charter of

Selections from the Magna Carta

The vast majority of the Magna Carta is devoted not to bold statements about the rights of mankind, but rather to the minutiae of aristocratic life in 13th-century Britain. Among the very important issues discussed:

Whether or not widows should be forced to marry (they should not, although they may have to leave their dead husband's house forty days after his death).

The rights of men "who live outside the forest" (they should not have to appear before courts inside the forest).

And, of course, no Great Charter would be complete without a little misogyny. The entire 54th clause of the Magna Carta: "No one shall be arrested or imprisoned upon the appeal of a woman for the death of anyone except her husband."

Liberties," which granted some measure of freedom and liberty to British citizens, just so long as they were English and male and of noble birth. But this document was conferred upon the people, not extracted from the king, which made it revocable (indeed, monarchs rarely abided by it).

A century later, the king was named John, and fortunately for the cause of liberty, he was awful at being king. John took the throne by murdering his nephew, and then proceeded to lose a war to the French, and finally threw a hissy fit when the Catholic Church appointed an archbishop of Canterbury whom John didn't like.

The barons of England could rarely agree on anything back then, but they did agree that John was an idiot. So, they banded together and stormed London. Soon afterward, in the meadow at Runnymede (which to us sounds like a kind of British food), they cajoled King

The Cutting Room Floor

In the centuries after the Magna Carta took effect, the power of the British monarchy actually increased. By the 16th century, the document was thought so insignificant that it isn't even mentioned in Shakespeare's play *King John*. Too bad, since it might have improved the play—one of Shakespeare's lesser efforts.

John into signing a document that granted them increased power and freedoms, and gave the Church a measure of autonomy. Consisting of a preamble and 63 clauses, the Magna Carta's most important clause, to the barons at least, was number 61, which gave them the right to overrule the king if 25 barons agreed he was violating the Magna Carta. But its lasting importance lay in requiring fair trials before sentencing and affirming the right to dissent.

The document was repeatedly reissued until it became permanent in 1225. While the aristocracy sometimes used it in negotiations with monarchs, its primary importance was not to the 13th century but to the 18th, when those seeking liberty and representative government turned to it when drafting their own great charters.

Conversation Starters

◆ Believe it or not, the original Magna Carta has been lost. But about 17 copies dating from 1297 or earlier survive, and early copies of the Magna Carta are among the most sought after rare documents in the world. In fact, very few are in private hands. One notable exception is that owned by the chart-loving, big-eared, former presidential candidate/billionaire Ross Perot.

◆ In those days, anyone who lent money with interest could be excommunicated by the Catholic Church for the sin of usury. So, it's no wonder that Jewish people became the primary lenders in medieval Europe. But debtors in default often brought their cases before Church courts, where the loans were usually declared illegal and the debts erased. As such, the Magna Carta was the first document in Britain to give some recourse to Jewish lenders, although it did annul some debts in the event of a debtor's death.

◆ Technically, one should always say "Magna Carta" and never "*the* Magna Carta," because there is no definite article in Latin. Most reference sources adhere to this rule, but we're ignoring it due to our principled and deeply held belief that "the Magna Carta" just sounds better.

Martini

Name-dropping: Martini (mar-TEE-nee) (developed around 1900). These days, of course, you can get anything in a martini glass: apple martinis, chocolate martinis, serve-your-own mashed potatoes. But the original martini is the only cocktail you'll ever need to look sophisticated. Probably the single best—or worst, if you hate olives—result of Prohibition in America.

When to Drop Your Knowledge: Well, if your angle is stuffy pretension, you can bring up the *real* martini whenever people start drinking wimpy *vodka* martinis. But even if you're *not* an obnoxious purist when it comes to drinking, you'll have ample opportunity to talk martinis. People love to talk about drinking when they're drinking.

The Basics

It started with the Martinez. Back in 19th-century California, the Martinez was a drink featuring a shot of gin and two shots of dry vermouth, cherry juice, and a lemon slice. Around 1900, someone got an idea: "If we had more gin than vermouth and got rid of the cherry juice, we could sure get drunk a lot faster." Not a bad idea. Add an olive, and the martini was born! As H. L. Mencken once put it, the martini is "the only American invention as perfect as the sonnet."

Traditionally, a martini consists of 1.5 ounces of gin, .5 ounce of dry vermouth, ice, and an olive (other acceptable

The Quotable Martini

"One martini is all right, two is too many, and three is not enough." —James Thurber

"I like to have a martini/Two at the very most./Three, I'm under the table/Four, I'm under the host." —Dorothy Parker

"Happiness is a dry martini and a good woman. Or a bad woman." —George Burns

Shaken, Not Stirred

James Bond is perhaps the most famous of all martini drinkers. His trademark order, "shaken, not stirred," has been a catchphrase for decades. Only one problem: James Bond does not drink martinis, which contain only gin, vermouth, and an olive. *Real* martinis are generally best stirred, not shaken. But Bond drinks *vodka* martinis. Martini snobs will tell you it's the equivalent of racing in the Tour de France on a bike

garnishes include lemon twists, capers, or cocktail onions). The drink quickly gained in popularity, but it wasn't until Prohibition that the martini became *the* American cocktail. When booze was legal, Americans on the whole preferred drinking whiskey. But it takes skill and time to make good whiskey, whereas pretty much any sap with a bathtub in the woods can make a few gallons of bathtub gin. Vermouth's central purpose in the Prohibition days was to improve the taste of the gin.

When Prohibition ended, gin stopped tasting like burning gasoline. That's when the dry martini truly came into fashion. A dry martini has a mere splash of vermouth, and soon, martinis were so incredibly dry that they were often just gin on the rocks with an olive. For those who want just a hint of vermouth, we suggest "coating the cubes," which with a banana seat. Shaking a drink does cool it faster, though, which is necessary because warm vodka martinis taste like olive-flavored lighter fluid. And Bond clearly knew this. In Ian Fleming's first Bond novel, *Casino Royale* (1953), Bond tells the bartender: "Shake it very well until it's ice cold." Today, the vodka martini is probably more popular than the original, perhaps due in part to 007, but mostly because gin is an acquired taste that many people just never really acquire.

As previously noted, martinis are considered best when stirred. However, it's possible that shaken martinis might improve your longevity. A recent study in the *British Medical Journal* argued that shaken martinis may release more antioxidants than stirred martinis. The antioxidant properties of alcohol are thought to help prevent heart attacks and stroke. But if you really want antioxidants (and still want to get drunk) avoid martinis altogether and drink some red wine.

involves pouring vermouth over the ice and then pouring the vermouth back into the bottle.

After falling out of favor in the 1970s, the martini has made a comeback. And although martini purists scoff at the endless varieties, the old standby remains a cocktail party favorite.

Conversation Starters

◆ Ernest Hemingway called his martini recipe a "Montgomery." It featured a gin to vermouth ratio of 15:1. Hemingway named it after Field Marshal Bernard Montgomery—whom, the joke went, required a 15:1 advantage before he'd go into battle.

◆ Early film actor W. C. Fields is today remembered primarily for being extremely funny about his intractable alcoholism. This is a man who drank two bottles of gin a day *when he was in rehab*. Fields always kept a thermos filled with a gigantic martini on the sets of his films, but he invariably referred to it as "pineapple juice." One day, a member of the film crew decided to play a prank on Fields. After taking a swig from the thermos, Fields cried, "Somebody put pineapple juice in my pineapple juice!"

◆ During World War II, French vermouth became exceedingly rare in Britain, but noted prime minister and alcoholic Winston Churchill wasn't going to let that stop him from drinking his martinis. Instead, it is said that he took his martinis *very, very* dry: He poured himself a glass of gin over ice, plopped an olive in the glass, and then tipped his glass in the direction of France.

◆ Speaking of Churchill and booze: Most people know the "I may be drunk, but I'll be sober tomorrow and you'll still be ugly" story, but our favorite Churchill boozing story goes like this: Lady Astor to Churchill: "Sir, if you were my husband, I would poison your drink." Churchill in response: "Madam, if you were my wife, I would drink it."

Alfred Nobel

Name-dropping: Alfred Bernhard Nobel (pronunciation: no-BELL) (1833–1896). A smart Swedish kid who just happened to have a deep and incontrovertible passion for blowing stuff up. And so it came to pass that the most widely respected peace prize in the world was paid for, basically, by explosives.

When to Drop Your Knowledge: It's admittedly unlikely that you'll ever be at a party with a Nobel laureate. But should it happen, you'll surely look dumb if you don't have anything to say. Also, knowledge of Nobel's exploits can be helpful when trying to explain your boorish behavior late in the evening. "Sorry," you can say, "I'm more bombed than Alfred Nobel's factory in 1864."

The Basics

Like a lot of kids, the young Alfred Nobel loved blowing stuff up. But little Alfie just never grew up. As a young man, Nobel began experimenting with liquid nitroglycerin, an explosive compound that, while highly unstable, was much better at blowing things up than anything previously invented. In 1862, he built a factory to manufacture and sell nitroglycerin, and shortly after, he invented the first semisafe detonator for it. Later, he also invented the blasting cap, which proved a godsend for miners, and ushered in the modern era of explosives.

But nitroglycerin was by no means *safe.* In fact, Nobel's own factory blew up in 1864, killing his younger brother,

Worst Nobel Prize Winner Ever

Once a Nobel Prize is given, it cannot be revoked. Now and again, the award goes to someone who maybe did not deserve it, but the most undeserving winner has to be Antonio Egas Moniz, the Portuguese physician who won the prize for medicine in 1946 for inventing—yes—the leucotomy prefrontal (lobotomy).

Egas Moniz's surgery consisted of—if we may simplify it a bit—drilling a few holes in a patient's skull and then repeatedly stabbing the patient in the brain. The lobotomy seemed to be successful at curing people of schizophrenic and paranoid psychoses, but they proved to have fairly serious side effects, such as "becoming a vegetable" and "becoming dead." Although lobotomies are rare today, thanks to an improved understanding of mental illness and psychosis treatments, they're still occasionally performed in some parts of the world.

Emil. But Alfred still believed in the power of explosives, and in 1867, he invented, half by accident, a much safer compound that he named, "dynamite." The big "D" made Alfred ridiculously wealthy, and the innovative Swede soon owned a host of factories around Europe.

Despite all this, however, Nobel never married. He seemed to find explosives more interesting than any woman, so he left no heirs. Instead, he put the bulk of his fortune (more than $9 million) to establishing a series of prizes. These awards—presented annually in the fields of physics, chemistry, economics, physiology or medicine, literature, and peace making—quickly became the most prestigious intellectual prizes in the world. In the end, Nobel would be better remembered for his prize than for his explosives used in modern warfare—which may be the very reason Nobel's will ordered that the prize be named for him.

REPORTS OF MY DEATH . . .

Alfred's brother Ludvig died in Cannes, France. French newspapers, never renowned for their fact-checking, somehow mixed up Ludvig and Alfred, and ended up running obituaries for Alfred instead. The headline in one paper read: "The Merchant of Death Is Dead." Some historians have speculated that Alfred was so horrified by the thought that he might be remembered only as a merchant of death that he decided to create a trust fund for the prizes—which would mean that we owe the Nobel Prize to poor reporting.

YOU COULD BE A WINNER!

Your best chance to win a Nobel Prize is to find work as an economist. The economics award usually goes to more than one person, and frequently goes to Americans. But whether you're an economist, a poet, or just a schmuck who wouldn't mind winning the Peace Prize (if Henry Kissinger can win it, then, by God, why can't you?), here's how to make it happen:

1. Get nominated. Unfortunately, you cannot nominate yourself. Nor can you have just anyone nominate you. Unless you know some former Nobel winners or the president of a sovereign nation, your best bet is to find a college professor teaching the subject in question and have her nominate you. Make sure to be nominated by February 1.

2. From here on out, you'd better be either exceptionally talented or exceptionally lucky, because the Nobel Committees are notoriously averse to bribery. But *if* they choose you . . .

3. The committee will submit your nomination to the Royal Swedish Academy of Sciences. Usually, the academy agrees with the committee's nomination, in which case you'll get an early-morning call sometime in October to inform you that you've won the Nobel Prize. Just be sure to thank **mental**_floss in your speech.

Conversation Starters

◆ According to Dr. Donald W. Goodwin's book *Alcohol and the Writer*, half the Americans who won the Nobel Prize for Literature were most likely alcoholics. The drunks: Sinclair Lewis, Eugene O'Neill, John Steinbeck, William Faulkner, and Ernest Hemingway. The nondrunks: Pearl Buck, Saul Bellow, and Toni Morrison.

◆ Mohandas Gandhi—Gandhi!!!—never won the Nobel Prize. Although nominated five times between 1937 and 1948, Gandhi was beaten out by the likes of Lord Edgar Algernon, R. G. Cecil, and Cordell Hull (who? our point exactly). After Gandhi's death, the Nobel Committee publicly expressed regret for the omission. And although posthumous awards aren't given, the Nobel Committee came as close as possible in 1948, the year Gandhi died, when they did not give out an award because "there was no suitable *living* candidate."

Pythagoras

Name-dropping: Pythagoras (pronunciation: pih-THAG-or-us) (c. 580–500 BCE). A man too famous for two names. See also Socrates, Plato, Sting.

Mathematikoi (pronunciation: MATH-ee-mat-ee-koi): The crazy kids who followed Pythagoras's crazy teachings.

Pythagorean theorem (just in case you need a refresher): Given a triangle with one 90-degree angle, with the shorter legs being *a* and *b,* and the hypotenuse being *c:* *a* squared + *b* squared = *c* squared.

When to Drop Your Knowledge: Obviously, Pythagoras will come in handy at a cocktail party with mathematicians—and if you find yourself at one of those, you'll need plenty of conversational ammunition. But the man behind the theorem might also be useful when hanging out with vegetarians, doctors, and even Stephen Hawking. Why? Read on.

The Basics

Very little is known about Pythagoras, except that the philosopher, mathematician, and quasi-cult leader almost certainly did not discover the Pythagorean theorem. Born on an island off the coast of Asia Minor, Pythagoras lived most of his life in Croton (in what is now southern Italy). More of a political and moral reformer than a mathematician or philosopher, Pythagoras formed a brotherhood called the *mathematikoi,* a kind of

Math Club for ancient Greece. The *mathematikoi* believed that numbers held the key to everything: music, poetry, philosophy, and the laws governing the workings of the universe. (As math club alums ourselves, we can report definitively that Pythagoras was incorrect: Numbers do not hold the key to getting a girlfriend.) Pythagoreanism was primarily a mystical religion (they believed in reincarnation and often sang hymns to Apollo).

Nonetheless, Pythagoras or one of his followers had several important mathematical insights. But it doesn't seem likely that they were the first to discover the equation we know today as the Pythagorean theorem. Many math historians now believe that the Egyptians used the same theorem in their construction projects a hundred years before Pythagoras was born. Further, the Indian mathematician Baudhayana (who frankly we're glad didn't get credit because "the Baudhayana theorem" just doesn't roll off the tongue) was also playing with those concepts way back in eighth-century BCE.

The Pythagoreans' greatest mathematical accomplishment was one that finally undermined his belief that whole numbers and their rations (i.e., 2, 2/3, etc.) could express

Music Man

Pythagoras believed that music was an audible expression of mathematical laws. Using intervals of pure fifths, Pythagoras created a method of tuning instruments that was popular with musicians up through the Renaissance. Unfortunately, in his lust to make music out of numbers, Pythagoras oversimplified the musical scale, creating finely tuned instruments that sounded awfully discordant. Today, you rarely hear Pythagorean-tuned instruments outside of authentic Shakespeare revivals. And trust us: If you do hear them, you'll rather wish you hadn't.

everything in math and the universe. A *mathematikoi* named Hippasus discovered that the square root of 2 was an irrational number—that is, it couldn't be expressed as a ratio of two whole numbers. Upon learning this, Pythagoras became so upset that he actually had Hippasus killed (the man didn't kid around when it came to numbers). As for mathematicians, they went ahead and pretended that Hippasus's discovery hadn't happened for more than a millennium, because they couldn't make any sense of it.

Oddly enough, Pythagoras's greatest contribution to math was to the *idea* of math. The first "pure mathematician," he was interested in numbers as abstractions instead of as practical qualities of math. So really, it's Pythagoras, at least in part, whose name we should all be cursing when recalling all that math on the SAT.

Conversation Starters

◆ The Hippocratic Oath's most quoted line, "First do no harm," originally comes not from the Greek physician Hippocrates but from the oath Pythagoras's followers took to join his sect.

◆ The Pythagoreans played the lyre to sick people in an attempt to cure them—which probably wasn't very effective.

◆ The Pythagoreans' belief that all music was numbers and all numbers were music might have had its roots in the uncommon but fascinating disorder synaesthesia. Synaesthetics intermingle the senses in their brain: They may see sounds or associate words with a taste or color. Or they might hear numbers, as Pythagoras seemed to.

◆ Pythagoras also believed that planets produced a harmonic sound called "the music of the spheres." Pythagoras didn't think the spinning planets made an audible sound; he merely believed that as they rotated around the earth, all heavenly spheres stayed in proportion to musical scales. That, as it turns out, is bunk. But the heavens *do* make sounds; radio telescopes have shown us that sunbursts sound like hisses and storms on Jupiter sound like popping popcorn.

◆ Proof that maybe your 10th-grade English teacher wasn't full of it; Pythagoreans regularly recited poetry together in hopes of improving their memory.

The Qur'an

Name-dropping: Qur'an (pronunciation: kuh-RAHN).
The holy book of Islam. Also spelled Koran.

Islam (pronunciation: iss-LAHM). Literally meaning
"submission," Islam is the religion.

Muslim (pronunciation: MOO-slim in the Arabic
world; generally MUZZ-lim in English). Literally meaning
"one who submits," a Muslim is a person who embraces Islam.

Muhammad (pronunciation: muh-HAHM-mud)
(570–632 HCE). The founder of Islam, to whom the
Qur'an was revealed.

When to Drop Your Knowledge: They say never to
discuss religion, sex, or politics at parties, but don't let
that stop you. Your knowledge of the Qur'an will allow
you to talk with great authority on religion, sex, *and*
politics all at once.

The Basics

When a young Meccan businessman named Muhammad first
heard the voice in 610, it said, "Recite." Like most people who
hear nonhuman voices, Muhammad was reluctant to do as the
voice said, possibly because it's hard to introduce your fellow
Meccans to a radically new monotheism by saying, "So, I've
been hearing this voice." But when Muhammad finally *did*
begin to recite what God was telling him through the Angel
Gabriel, people listened. Most believe that Muhammad

Extra Credit: POLYGAMY

Polygamy was the norm in pre-Islamic Arabia, and Muhammad himself had some seven wives during his lifetime. (He married some of them to cement treaties between tribes.) But the Qur'an asserts that male Muslims can marry four wives at most (prophets, obviously, are an exception). In the Bible, a lot of famous individuals had more than one wife, too, including Jacob, who had two, and Solomon, who had seven hundred. Although wealthy men—particularly in Saudi Arabia—still sometimes practice polygamy, it's become extremely rare.

Pillar Fight!

The Qur'an highlights five pillars of Islam. You're a Muslim if you commit to the first pillar; but if you do all five, you're a really *good* Muslim.

1. **Shahada.** Belief in the unity of God and the Prophethood of Muhammad.
2. **Salat.** Although Muslims can and do pray whenever they want, there are five

himself was illiterate, but the revelations that came through him over the next 20 years were beautiful, intricately rhythmic Arabic. They advertised one God to a people that had always believed in many—a God of love and justice, whose name in Arabic is Allah. When these revelations were written down and gathered together, they came to be known as the Qur'an.

Unlike sacred texts from most religious traditions, the Qur'an is considered to be the actual, literal word of God. And it isn't organized into a chronological narrative. Instead, the Qur'an is organized roughly according to the length of its chapters, called *surahs*—with the longest coming first and the shortest last. In total length, the Qur'an is about as long as the New Testament.

Because of its lack of traditional narrative structure, the Qur'an doesn't make for the easiest reading

COCKTAIL PARTY CHEAT SHEETS

ritualized prayers each day: at dawn, midmorning, noon, midday, and sunset.

3. **Ramadan.** Those who are old enough and healthy enough fast during daylight hours during the month of Ramadan (because the Islamic calendar is lunar, Ramadan moves from season to season). Fasting means no food or liquid—and for smokers, no cigarettes.

4. **Zakat.** All Muslims are obligated to give a percentage of their income in alms to the poor.

5. **Hajj.** All Muslims who can afford the journey should make the pilgrimage to Mecca (in Saudi Arabia), the holiest city in Islam, at least once.

While the Qur'an is the supreme authority when it comes to Islamic law, the Hadiths are a collection of stories about and sayings by the prophet, collected by his companions. The Hadiths, some of which are considered unreliable by Muslims and secular historians alike, have become particularly important in places like Iran, where every facet of the law requires a religious justification.

in English. So, you're well advised to just trust us when we say that the Qur'an, in Arabic, is ceaselessly beautiful. Its overarching message is the unity of God, known in Arabic as *Tauhid*. This one God will one day judge all people by their faith and their actions. Of course, the actions that you should take are covered in depth in the Qur'an—you shouldn't eat pork; you shouldn't charge interest on loans; you should treat people as you wish to be treated.

If this sounds remarkably Judeo-Christian—well, it is. And in the interest of bringing people together, we're inventing a new term: Chrislamo-Judaic. The Qur'an retells many stories from Jewish and Christian mythology, featuring such famous biblical characters as Abraham, Isaac, Moses, and Jesus.

Conversation Starters

◆ Can you be a Muslim *and* a Jew? Well, not so much now, but there was a time in which the identities were not mutually exclusive. That's right; there were once Jews for Muhammad (although they didn't hand out pamphlets on street corners). In the seventh century, some Jews embraced Muhammad's status as a prophet without abandoning their own conception of Judaism. (Most of the major Jewish prophets, including Abraham and Moses, are prophets in Islam as well.)

◆ Jesus is a major prophet in Islam and is discussed periodically in the Qur'an (his Arabic name is Isa). But the Qur'anic Jesus was not crucified—God takes him up to heaven just *before* his crucifixion is to take place.

◆ Drinking alcohol, or ingesting any intoxicant, is forbidden by the Qur'an. (The same is true of Buddhism.) It's hard to find booze in much of the Islamic world, and even when you can, you may wish you hadn't. The Egyptians were among the first to brew beer, but their state-run brewery today reputedly produces the worst-quality brew on the planet.

◆ The Qur'an in its current form was not collected and authorized until nearly 20 years after Muhammad's death in 632. Uthman, the third caliph of the Arab empire after Muhammad's passing, brought scholars together to compare notes, and then decided on the exact language and organization of the document.

Rosetta Stone

Name-dropping: Rosetta Stone (pronunciation: Roh-ZEH-tuh) (discovered in 1799). A single ancient stone discovered near the city of Rosetta in Egypt (one does begin to wish after a while that people would be more creative in naming their discoveries) that contains the same text written in two languages (Egyptian and Greek) in three scripts (Greek, demotic, and hieroglyphic). Using a magical decoder ring, or possibly their wits, linguists eventually learned how to decipher hieroglyphics from it.

When to Drop Your Knowledge: At the company Christmas party, when the close-talking, whiskey-gulping manager from Accounts Receivable starts slurring his words to the degree that he is no longer speaking a language that can technically be classified as English, you can just smile brightly, give a bit of Rosetta Stone history, say that you're off to track down one that translates Drunk Talk, and take your leave of him.

The Basics

For centuries, Egyptian hieroglyphics were absolutely incomprehensible. Pyramid, crow, lion, squiggly line—what? But in 1799, the Rosetta Stone was discovered. Part of the stone was inscribed in ancient Greek, which everybody worth their salt could read back in 1799. The Greek was a (pretty boring, really) decree affirming loyalty to Emperor Ptolemy V (who at that time was all of 13 years old). Beside the Greek, the same decree was repeated in ancient Egypt's demotic script, and beside that, in hieroglyphics. Problem solved, right?

Not quite. Although the Rosetta Stone was the rare puzzle whose solution had actual consequences for our understanding of history—imagine if you could become famous for finishing one *New York Times* crossword puzzle—it proved considerably more complicated than a Jumble or a Rubik's cube.

The first person to make any headway with the Rosetta Stone was not a linguist but a physicist. Thomas Young proved that a certain set of hieroglyphics seemed to align with the Greek rendering for Ptolemy, and by observing the direction in which the bird characters faced (really), Young figured out the direction in which to read the hieroglyphics.

The central hindrance remained that scholars believed particular pictographs stood for ideas (i.e., that the lion meant the word *war*). It was Frenchman John-François Champollion who finished unraveling the mystery

The Rosetta Project

Lest humans (or aliens!) of the future have to suffer the way Champollion did, we will soon have parallel texts recorded in 1,000 languages. Begun in 2000, the Rosetta Project, a collaboration among linguists worldwide, intends to etch the 1,000 parallel texts into nickel alloy plates that are believed to last 2,000 years. The creators of the project argue that between 50 and 90 percent of the world's current languages will disappear in the next century due to ever-increasing globalization.

in 1824, when he established that some hieroglyphs were syllables and others letters of a kind of alphabet. Upon realizing that hieroglyphics were a phonetic script, Champollion is said to have fainted for five entire days (although to be fair, he was generally kind of a drama queen). Upon awaking, supposedly, he used the few hieroglyphs in "Ptolemy" to painstakingly translate the entire Rosetta Stone. The Stone, in turn, allowed scholars to understand the whole body of hieroglyphic literature, from that of the Great Pyramids to that of crumbling papyri.

YOU'RE NOT GETTING IT BACK!

Recently, formerly colonized nations have begun noting that a lot of their priceless treasures seem to be located in European museums. And that, according to the once colonized, seems rather akin to stealing. In 2005, Egypt formally requested that the British Museum return the Rosetta Stone to its native land. But British law prevents the museum from giving up anything in its collection (even items looted by the Nazis that ended up in Britain). So theoretically, if an employee of the British Museum wrenched a lollipop from the tiny hands of Little Orphan Annie and then put that lollipop in the museum's collection, it could—literally—not legally be returned to poor Annie. As for the Rosetta Stone dispute, it has yet to be settled.

Conversation Starters

◆ Some scholars now argue that Champollion wasn't the first to crack the Rosetta Stone's secrets at all. A London researcher argues that Arabic alchemist Abu Bakr Ahmad Ibn Wahshiya, whose name is equally long in pictographs, translated hieroglyphics using the Rosetta Stone nearly 1,000 years ago.

◆ Aside from helping to decode the Rosetta Stone, physicist Thomas Young also became a prominent advocate for the theory that light was waves, not streams of particles, as Newton claimed. (Einstein proved that both Young and Newton were right: Apparently, light behaves both as waves *and* as particles, which is the kind of idea that makes our heads hurt.)

◆ While most of us are content to leave whiskey at Jim Morrison's tomb in Paris, linguistically inclined visitors to Champillion's grave in Paris often leave sheets of papyrus at the tomb to honor his accomplishment.

ar-Rumi

Name-dropping: Jalal ad-Din ar-Rumi (pronunciation: juh-LAHL ahd-DINN ahr-ROO-mee) (1207–1273 CE). Sufi poet whose evocative verse earned him fans the world over during his life, and has kept him in print in dozens of languages ever since. Also, the best-selling poet overall in America in the 1980s and 1990s. (Sorry, Jewel.)

Sufism: (pronunciation: SOO-fizm). Islamic mysticism in which worshippers seek oneness with God.

When to Drop Your Knowledge: Rumi knew his way around the love poem (he composed some 30,000 verses of love poetry), so he can be of vital assistance when trying to woo someone at the tail end of a party. Where Spanish fly and Love Potion #9 will inevitably fail, Rumi will likely succeed.

The Basics

Rumi's father was a teacher and mystic in present-day Turkey, and when his dad died in 1231, Rumi decided to take up the family business. He was only 24, but he was soon respected for the depth of his study. In fact, Rumi was tutored by some of the greatest Islamic thinkers of the time, including Ibn al-'Arabi, who is Rumi's only rival for the title of "Greatest Sufi Ever."

Although Sufism, the mystical sect of Islam that seeks *Fana*, or annihilation into God, had been around in some form since

The Quotable Rumi

If only he'd lived to be about 800, Rumi would be *stinking rich*. The poet Coleman Barks's translations of Rumi have sold more than 600,000 copies (poet laureate and general poetry superstar Billy Collins, by contrast, sold 55,000 copies of his last book). As Barks himself sheepishly admits in the preface to one of his translations, "I have sold too many books."

On Love: "This is love: to fly toward a secret sky, to cause a hundred veils to fall each moment. First to let go of life. Finally, to take a step without feet."

On Love: "Lovers don't finally meet somewhere. They're in each other all along."

On Love: "Only from the heart can you touch the sky."

On Making Waterwheel Metaphors Sexy: "I become a waterwheel, turning and tasting you as long as water moves."

the very beginnings of Islam, it was coming into its own in the 13th century. Grand philosophies of Qur'anic interpretation, meditative prayer, and trance-inducing rituals were codified, and many people sought out spiritual experiences through Sufi leaders. So Rumi likely would have had a good and quiet life as a Sufi teacher had he not crossed paths with a wandering, unkempt mystic named Shams ad-Din (literally, "the Sun of Religion").

Shams became Rumi's spiritual adviser, and Rumi fell for Shams like no one has ever fallen for anybody. Their love—which may or may not have involved a romantic relationship—consumed Rumi, leading him to neglect his duties as a teacher so that he could spend all his time with Shams. In the end, Rumi would write some 30,000 verses about the stages of his love for Shams. And just as Sufis seek unification with the divine, Rumi sought (and found) unification with

Shams—so much so that Rumi began using the pen name "Shams."

The great strengths of Rumi's poems are the use of everyday descriptions and a personal, confessional tone rarely before seen in Persian poetry. Poetic technique never overshadows Rumi's passion, and that is why he remains read today while most of the classic Persian poets do not. Rumi's poems (at least in their original Persian) are also endearingly rhythmic, lending credence to the legend that he wrote them while listening to goldsmiths' hammering.

Unfortunately, his love affair with Shams was short-lived. His family had a business to run—albeit a mystical-union-with-God business—and having their best teacher staring dreamily into the eyes of some unkempt dervish all day was no good. So members of Rumi's family had Shams killed in 1247.

Rumi's next and final love was for an illiterate goldsmith, Salah ad-Din Zarkub, who had long been Rumi's disciple, and who inspired Rumi to write his great philosopho-religio-poetic (we just made that up) work, the *Masnavi-ye Ma'navi*. The six-volume poem is considered by many Muslims to be more important than any book save the Qur'an. Full of lengthy tangents and twisting narratives, the *Masnavi* is both a guide to divine love and a story of experiencing that love.

Conversation Starters

◆ Although Rumi is often viewed in the West as a mystical-poet-who-transcended-religion type, he was in fact quite religious and played an important role in spreading Islam into Asia Minor.

◆ Rumi's funeral was one of the more impressive interfaith gatherings of antiquity. It's said that Muslims, Christians, Jews, Hindus, and Buddhists were all in attendance.

◆ The Ellen DeGeneres of his day, Rumi brought dance to the forefront of Islamic ritual. He is said to have danced all night after meeting Shams, and the Sufi order he founded, the *Mawlawiyah*, was famous for the dance they did as part of prayer. European observers called them "whirling dervishes," a term that continues to be a popular (if somewhat inaccurate) description of Sufis.

◆ The phrase "whirling dervishes" may have lasted, but the *Mevleviyah* themselves have struggled. The radically secularist Turkish government disbanded all Sufi orders in 1925, and the *Mevleviyah* had no real presence outside of Turkey.

Santa Claus

Name-dropping: Santa Claus (aka Sinterklaas, Kriss Kringle, Jolly St. Nick—the guy's got more pseudonyms than a third-rate romance novelist). You might also know him as Saint Nicholas, bishop of Myra (who lived and died sometime during the fourth century CE)

When to Use Your Knowledge: Well, whatever you do, don't use it around kids. The world is hard enough for children without knowing the dark truths of Santology. But your newfound knowledge of all things Santa should be a huge hit at the office Christmas party.

The Basics

Yes, Virginia, there is a Santa Claus—or was, anyway. His name was Nicholas, and during the fourth century CE, he was bishop of Myra (a city in Turkey, and consequently, a bit of a walk from the North Pole). Little is known of Nicholas's life, but he was apparently imprisoned for his faith until the emperor Constantine converted to Christianity in 312. Nicholas also probably attended the influential Council of Nicea in 325, at which the books of the Bible were once and for all decided upon.

As bishop, Nicholas gained a reputation as a friend of the people, and after his death, he gained popularity as a patron saint, protecting everyone from sailors to children. In fact, by the 11th century, he was one of Europe's most popular saints.

But how did the celibate Turkish bishop end up as a fat white guy who was shacked up with a Mrs. in the North Pole?

Well, Nicholas's patronage of children led many European families to give gifts (like candy, not like dual-exhaust scale-model electric-powered Hummers) to their kids on his feast day, December 6. The tradition was especially popular with the Dutch, who brought the custom over to New York in the 17th century. And since the Dutch called St. Nick Sinterklaas, slowly, St. Nicholas's feast day became conflated with Christmas, and Sinterklaas became Santa Claus.

But Santa's big break came in 1822 with the publication of Clement Clarke Moore's poem, "A Visit from St. Nicholas" (now known as " 'Twas the Night Before Christmas"). The poem was such a huge hit that it single-handedly created many facets of the Santa myth, including the reindeer, the North Pole, and Santa's talent for squeezing through chimneys.

Not So Jolly St. Nick

Nicholas had a reputation for kindness and benevolence, but he sure hated paganism. After the Roman emperor Constantine converted to Christianity, Nicholas personally supervised the destruction of the most beautiful structure in his diocese, the Temple to Artemis. Nicholas also destroyed all the pagan icons in Myra, leading us to wonder how he'd feel about having become a big, fat, reindeer-driving icon himself.

By the mid-19th century, Santa had his current job, but it wasn't until the Civil War that he landed his world-famous outfit. In 1863, a cartoonist named Thomas Nast, who incidentally also drew the first version of the Uncle Sam we recognize today, published a drawing of a fat, bearded man with a thick fur suit in *Harper's*

Very Merry Math

Many children figure out the nonexistence of Santa Claus when they begin to contemplate the enormity of his task. And, indeed, Santa would need some rocket-powered reindeer: Assuming the world contains two billion households and Santa visits every one over the course of 24 hours, he would have to travel at a rate of 8,000,000 meters per second, leaving him precious little time to dip cookies in milk.

Weekly. Over the next 20 years, Nast's annual Santa portraits became a staple in *Harper's.*

The Santa brand grew further with help from the masters of marketing: Coca-Cola. In the 1930s, illustrator Haddon Sundblom drew a series of advertisements featuring a jolly, red-suited Santa drinking Coca-Cola. The campaign helped popularize Coke as a drink for all seasons (it was previously most popular in the summertime), but it also cemented Santa as a universal, and completely secular, American icon. Santa drinking a Coke marked the ultimate triumph of secular commercialism over piety and generosity—and Christmas has been more and more fun ever since.

Conversation Starters

◆ St. Nicholas's list of patronages is one of the longest in all Christendom. His connection to children led to his role as Santa, but Nicholas also watches over notaries, pharmacists, poets, soldiers, and the imprisoned, among many others. In fact, he's such a versatile saint that he also serves as a patron for both prostitutes *and* virgins. (Honestly.)

◆ There's long been a theory that Clement Clarke Moore did not write "'Twas the Night Before Christmas," but plagiarized it from obscure poet Henry Livingston Jr. The notion gained credibility when literature professor Don Foster, who utilized computer software to out Joe Klein as the author of the previously anonymous *Primary Colors*, claimed that Moore's writing style was utterly incongruent with the classic Christmas poem. Moore still has plenty of defenders—but it's quite possible the man who helped invent the modern Santa was a sham.

◆ In Greece, the Santa role is still sometimes played by St. Basil the Great, who delivers presents not on Christmas but New Year's (his feast day) riding atop a donkey. Basil, who lived about the same time as St. Nicholas, came from a family of saints: The Eastern Orthodox Church also sainted his mother, grandmother, sister, and two of his brothers.

⚓ Seven Wonders of the Ancient World

Name-dropping: *Ephesus* (pronunciation: EH-fuh-suss). Greek city no longer in existence.

Halicarnassus (pronunciation: Hal-ee-car-NASS-uss). Asia Minor city no longer in existence.

Babylon (pronunciation: like Babylon 5 sans the 5). Ancient Mesopotamian city and former seat of the Babylonian Empire. No longer in existence.

Rhodes (pronunciation: like roads). Island chronologically controlled by the Greeks, the Persians, the Greeks, the Romans, the Byzantines, the Turks, the Italians, Nazi Germany, and—finally—the Greeks again.

Alexandria (pronunciation: al-eggs-ZAN-dree-uh). Egyptian city (still exists!).

Olympia (pronunciation: like the town in Washington). Greek home to the original Olympics.

Giza (pronunciation: GEE-zuh). Ancient city known almost exclusively for its pyramids. Read on.

When to Drop Your Knowledge: When complimenting your host on a hanging-gardens-of-spinach-dip display, or chatting about the Statue of Liberty, or attending a cocktail party hosted by a couple living in a lighthouse, or anytime mausoleums come up.

The Basics

For whatever reason, Greek historians made more lists than obsessive-compulsive housewives. And one of their favorite topics was Wonders of the World. The lists didn't all include seven wonders, and didn't always agree (some wonders, like the walls of the city of Babylon, just didn't make the cut). By the sixth century CE, though, a standard list had emerged—the same one we use today:

THE GREAT PYRAMID OF GIZA

> **Quotable**
>
> According to a popular Arab proverb, "Man fears time, but time fears only the Pyramids."

The Empire State Building was the world's tallest building for 40 years (from 1931 to 1971). That seems impressive until you consider that, at 481 feet high, the Great Pyramid of Giza was the world's tallest building for more than 4,000 years (from around 2560 BCE until the 19th century CE).

Wonderment Level: ★★★★★ The Great Pyramid gets full marks, if only because it's the only ancient wonder still standing.

THE LIGHTHOUSE OF ALEXANDRIA

The very first lighthouse, it guided ships to the port of Alexandria (named for, and by, Alexander the Great) using a constantly burning fire that was reflected out to sea by a large mirror. The lighthouse was damaged by an earthquake in 1303 CE and collapsed soon after.

Wonderment Level: ★★★★ It was, for a time, the world's second-tallest structure.

THE STATUE OF ZEUS AT OLYMPIA

One of those ancient wonders that seems to have been picked by the Greeks because it was created by Greeks, the statue of the bearded, lightning-hurling king of the gods, was built near the site of the Olympic games.

Wonderment Level: ★ We know the Greeks invented democracy and everything, but that doesn't give them license to go and label their every statue a wonder.

THE TEMPLE OF ARTEMIS AT EPHESUS

Twice as big as the Parthenon, the Temple of Artemis is relatively unknown today. Its 127 columns, each 60 feet tall, were all destroyed in 262 CE by the Goths.

Wonderment Level: ★★★

Lighthouse Legends

Remember killing ants with a well-aimed magnifying glass on a sunny day? Well, imagine that phenomenon on a much larger scale. Legend has it that the huge mirror at the Alexandrian Lighthouse was used to concentrate and reflect sunlight on enemy ships, causing them to burst into flames. (If you're wondering whether that is actually possible: No. It isn't. But good story, ancient Alexandria!)

Today, Ephesus is primarily remembered for a letter, which ended up in the Bible, written to its residents by the Apostle Paul. But it was also one heck of a temple.

THE HANGING GARDENS OF BABYLON

Created by King Nebuchadnezzar II, the Hanging Gardens of Babylon were built atop cube-shaped columns, and comprised dozens of high, beautifully landscaped terraces. The green-thumbed touches all gave Babylon the illusion of topography, which was exactly the point: Supposedly, Nebuchadnezzar's wife was homesick for the mountainous land of her childhood, so he built them to cheer her up.

Wonderment Level: ★★★★ While definitely remarkable, the gardens weren't nearly as impressive as their irrigation system, which required huge and exceedingly complex water-wheels (if you've ever been to Disney World, think Swiss Family Robinson).

THE MAUSOLEUM AT HALICARNASSUS

In 323 BCE, a minor king of a minor kingdom in Asia Minor died. His name was Mausolus, and his wife, who, incidentally, was also his sister, was devastated. (You would be, too, if you lost your brother and your husband all at once.) She built him a huge stone tomb that was so impressive that Mausolus, who would have otherwise been forgotten, lived on as a word: *mausoleum*.

> The Wonders of the World didn't exactly cover the earth: The farthest apart (Zeus and the Hanging Gardens) were separated by only about 1,200 miles. That's approximately the distance between Boston and St. Louis.

Wonderment Level: ★★ Three stars for the impressive tomb. Subtract one star for marrying your sister.

THE COLOSSUS OF RHODES

Another Greek statue passing as a wonder of the world because it was built by Greeks? Well, yes. In 282 BCE, the people on the island of Rhodes erected a 110-foot bronze monument to their patron god, Helios. With its pointy crown, the statue bears a striking resemblance to another famous statue situated near an island city: the Statue of Liberty, which was actually modeled on the Colossus.

Wonderment Level: ★★ It may have inspired Lady Liberty, but the Colossus only stood for 55 years.

Conversation Starters

◆ From head to toe, the modern-day Statue of Liberty is nearly the same height as the ancient Colossus of Rhodes.

◆ Although the Lighthouse of Alexandria was built on the island of Pharos, in its heyday, Pharos was sort of the Coney Island of Alexandria. Visitors could climb to the top of the lighthouse to enjoy the view, and could even purchase snacks on its ground floor.

◆ A pharaoh named Khufu ordered the building of the Great Pyramid in honor of, uh, himself. Khufu, incidentally, wasn't the best pharaoh who ever came down the pike. According to the Greek historian Herodotus, he "brought the country into all kinds of misery." Maybe, but he's been great for tourism ever since!

◆ Crusaders occupied Halicarnassus in 1522. Fearing an attack from the Turks, however, the Crusaders showed the kind of Christian piety and kindness for which they are famous, and decided to reinforce the walls of the town by stealing stones. But where could they get such fine materials? From the ruins of the town's famed mausoleum, of course! By the time their foraging was complete, the mausoleum's foundation was completely unrecognizable.

Tanakh

Name-dropping: *Tanakh* (pronunciation: tah-NOCK). Also known as the Hebrew Bible and often identified as the Old Testament, the *Tanakh* comprises the 24 books in the Hebrew canon read as scripture in Judaism.

When to Drop Your Knowledge: Whenever anyone calls the Hebrew Bible the Old Testament, for starters. But your knowledge of the *Tanakh* is also sure to be a hit at bat and bar mitzvahs. Of course, you'll probably need the conversation to pass the time, because even though they mark the entrance into adulthood, the "bar" in bar mitzvah rarely stands for open bar.

The Basics

Tanakh is an acronym from the initial letters of the Hebrew words *Torah*, meaning "The Law," *Nevi'im*, meaning "Prophets," and *Ketuvim* (meaning "Writings"). These three categories of writing compose the Hebrew Bible, which most Christians know as the Old Testament.

The *Torah* includes the five books of Moses—Genesis, Exodus, Leviticus, Numbers, and Deuteronomy—which introduce the beginnings of human history (with Adam and Eve) and Jewish history (with Abraham, who both Jews and Muslims view as their patriarch). It is also the basis for most Jewish law. (Traditionally, the law of Moses is said to contain exactly 613 commandments.)

Talmud

The Talmud, which began to be recorded around 200 BCE, holds a place in Jewish tradition second only to the *Tanakh*. The work of many Rabbinic scholars, the Talmud includes law passed down orally as well as critical and interpretive commentary on scripture. The Talmudic authors sought to fill out the Jewish law outlined in the *Torah* so as to help people live holy and spiritual lives. Today, however, most Reform Jews and many others reject the Talmud as an excessively legalistic and sort of crushingly nonspiritual text. But Orthodox Jews in particular continue to adhere to the law as set forth in the Talmud.

The *Nevi'im* is the writings of the Prophets. From Joshua to Ezekiel, the Prophets exhorted the Jewish community to live up to their covenant with God as his chosen people. They promised, cajoled, and threatened. For much of Jewish history, there was disagreement about which prophets ought to be considered canonical, but a conference of rabbis around 100 CE set down the *Nevi'im* as we read it today.

The *Ketuvim* includes everything else. It includes the oddest, and arguably the most beautiful writing in the Christian and Jewish canon. Truly a miscellany, the *Ketuvim* includes history (Nehemiah), devotional poetry (the Psalms), prophecy that didn't end up in the *Nevi'im* (Daniel), disconcertingly erotic poetry (the Song of Songs), and the saddest story ever told (Job). The books of the *Ketuvim* were not canonized as a group, like the other two sections of the *Tanakh*, but instead were brought into the scriptures individually, usually because regular people liked them so much. This created the mishmash feel of the *Ketuvim*, but also ensured the enduring popularity of most of its books.

Although Christians reading the *Tanakh* usually see it as a kind of forerunner to the New Testament, and find within it prophecies about Jesus, it is read quite differently in Judaism. It is a testament to the remarkable survival and flourishing of a small band of people who believed in one God long before it was popular, who suffered persecution again and again but always emerged intact, and whose greatness lies not in their numbers but in their commitment to, and faith in, the one true God.

WHAT'S THE DIFFERENCE?
THE HEBREW BIBLE EDITION

So what's the difference between the Hebrew Bible and the Christian Old Testament? The Catholic Old Testament includes "the Apocrypha," several books that both Protestants and Jews decided weren't canonical. The Protestant Old Testament is identical, but the order of the books is different. Still, though, it's offensive to many Jewish people to call the Hebrew Bible the *Old* Testament, because it implies the existence of a *New* Testament, and Judaism does not believe in any such thing.

Conversation Starters

◆ Like many a Yugoslavian town name, the Hebrew text of the *Tanakh* originally contained only consonants. Pronunciation of words was passed down orally until the early Middle Ages, when diacritical marks were added to codify the pronunciation.

◆ In the Christian Old Testament, Kings, Samuel, and Chronicles are each divided into two books. This wasn't originally the case with the *Tanakh*, but the three books proved too long for the scrolls that early Christians used, so they divided them.

◆ Almost all of the *Tanakh* was composed in Hebrew. The exceptions consist of two words in Genesis, a sentence in Jeremiah, two in Ezra, and almost half the Book of David. These sections were all written in Aramaic, which was spoken by many Jews for millennia, and by the cast of *The Passion of the Christ* for a few months. By contrast, the New Testament was probably written entirely in ancient Greek, except for one sentence of Aramaic. In the Gospel According to Mark, Jesus' last words are recorded as the Aramaic *"elo'i elo'i lama sabachthani,"* or "My God, my God, why have you forsaken me?"

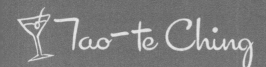
Tao-te Ching

Name-dropping: *Tao-te Ching* (pronunciation: dao de-ZHING). The holy scripture of Taoism (pronunciation: DAO-ism) compiled sometime before the third century BCE.

Lao-tzu (pronunciation: LAO-tsuh): Literally, "Old Man," "Lao-tzu" is both the same book as the *Tao-te Ching* and the name of the person who purportedly wrote it. If this strikes you as confusing, just wait. It gets worse.

When to Drop Your Knowledge: Fans of Chinese religion will obviously be pleased with your ability to intelligently discuss the Tao. But the surest cocktail party use for the *Tao-te Ching* is to calm down belligerent, verbose drunks. "To use words but rarely," you can quote to them, "is to be natural."

The Basics

The *Tao-te Ching*, originally known to its Chinese audience as *Lao-tzu*, is an extremely short, esoteric book of verse that, along with the works of Confucius, shaped Chinese philosophy and religion for two millennia. While Confucianism emphasized respect for authority, proper behavior, and building better communities through civilization, Taoism emphasized natural societies and, indeed, living in accordance with the world as it currently is.

This would be an excellent time to say what, exactly, the

The Tao of Everything

The *Tao-te Ching* itself espouses antimaterialistic values and a general opposition toward naked ambition. But this hasn't stopped authors from capitalizing on the inherent "cool factor" of Taoism to twist its fundamental beliefs into fame and profit.

The first, and generally least inaccurate, book in the *"Tao of"* genre was Benjamin Hoff's 1983 *The Tao of Pooh*, which argued that we should all be more Taoist, and also more like Winnie the Pooh. But after that, the *"Tao of"* books spiraled out of control. A selection of the several dozen *"Tao of"* books currently in print:

The Tao of Physics
The Tao of Leadership
The Tao of Equus
The Tao of Sobriety
The Tao of Photography
And, of course, that major American literary classic, *The Tao of Network Security Monitoring*.

Tao, means—but sadly, we can't. To quote the very first line of the *Tao-te Ching*: "The *Tao* that can be spoken of is not the eternal *Tao*." But that won't keep us from trying. *Tao* is often translated "the Way," and it's taken to mean the harmony of the cosmos. Our job, as people, is not to fight against that harmony, but instead, submit to it.

The *Tao-te Ching* is often considered an esoteric, mystical work, because it is rife with paradox. "My words are very easy to understand and very easy to put into practice, yet no one in the world can understand them or put them into practice," for instance, doesn't make much sense—at least not initially. But Taoism embraces such paradoxes and they often eventually prove sensical. Although "the strength of softness" may seem oxymoronical, Taoism takes the example of water: Although it flows with the stream and is exceedingly

The Tao of Who?

In all probability, Lao-tzu never existed. Tradition states that Lao-tzu was an older contemporary of Confucius (who was a historical person, and lived from 551 to 479 BCE). But most scholars believe that the *Tao-te Ching* was not a single work from a single person but rather a collection that was refined over the course of decades and possibly even centuries. Still, images of Lao-tzu—a bearded and happy man with a more-than-passing resemblance (skin color aside) to Yoda—abound.

soft, it has the power to slowly wear down earth and rock. The goal of the *Tao-te Ching* is to help people accept the inevitability of change and find a way to end the conflict that results from resistance to change. It's no wonder that most scholars believe it was authored during a tumultuous period of Chinese history marked by philosophical disagreements and warring factions battling for power.

Taoism first became popular in China in the late third century CE, and while neo-Confucianism remained the state religion until Mao Tse-tung made the state religion "worshipping me, Mao Tse-tung" in 1949, Taoism remained popular—and not necessarily mutually exclusive to Confucianism or Buddhism. In fact, it isn't uncommon for people in China to identify themselves as being both Buddhist and Taoist, or Confucianist and Taoist, or all three.

Conversation Starters

◆ Lots of people think *Taoism* means "being chill." After all, one of the guiding principles of the Tao is that one ought to go with the flow (the flow of the Tao, that is). But not all Taoists have been laid-back peacemakers. Far from it. Consider Guan Yu, the third-century Chinese general who is revered by Taoists as a guardian deity. Usually portrayed as a red-faced, sword-carrying warrior, Guan Yu helped overthrow the Han dynasty and is said to have severed more than a few heads.

◆ Early Taoists were obsessed with internal alchemy, which involves not the making of gold from base metals but rather refining one's body and mind in the hopes of achieving long life and, ideally, immortality. Some attempted to bring a permanent and immortal harmony to their body through exercise and dietary restrictions (as, really, we do today). But other Taoist alchemists invented potions and charms that they hoped would give them long life. Internal alchemy was occasionally fatal, and always ineffective—but then again, so was regular alchemy.

Nikola Tesla

The Basics

Nikola Tesla was a Serbian who emigrated to the United States in 1884. A contemporary of Edison and Westinghouse, both of whose names ended up in major corporations, Tesla was probably the greater inventor, but he ended up poverty-stricken and massively underappreciated. Tesla was responsible for the first practical use of alternating current (AC)—the electrical current that constantly reverses direction and is the heart of electric power for most of the world. Tesla's AC dynamos bested Edison's work with direct current by a wide margin, and AC eventually won the battle to light the world. But that's not all: Tesla also invented the Tesla coil—a gadget still used in radio and television transmission. He also messed around with early radar, neon, X-rays, and aircraft design. (This is what happens when you don't give kids a Nintendo.)

In some ways, Tesla was the prototypical immigrant success story: He arrived in America with four pennies, a few poems he'd written, and blueprints for a flying machine (that never got built). But by 1900, his greatest successes were behind him. Working out of his Colorado laboratory, Tesla had his version of a midlife crisis. His business ventures failed; he started to believe aliens from another planet were signaling earth; and most impressive, he claimed to have invented a "death ray" that could destroy thousands of airplanes from hundreds of miles away. (The death ray, like most of Tesla's later inventions, was never built for lack of funds.) His last years were even more depressing. Increasingly eccentric, Tesla lived in a series of New York hotel rooms, virtually friendless.

So how come he's not that famous? For one thing, he never patented most of his inventions. For another, other inventors took credit for many of Tesla's ideas and innovations, which is why major corporations are named after Edison and

Ignoble Nobels

In 1943 the Supreme Court invalidated most of the patents held by Italian inventor Guglielmo Marconi for radio equipment and gave Tesla credit for the invention of radio based on patents that predated Marconi's. Little good it did Tesla, though, because by that time Marconi had already won fame, riches, and a Nobel Prize for his "work," while Tesla was, um, dead. Tesla never won the Nobel—unless you count the one he got for Marconi. In fact, he was devastated in 1915 when rumors of a shared prize between him and Edison proved untrue. (The winners: William Henry Bragg and William Lawrence Bragg, for their work on X-ray crystallography. The Braggs, incidentally, remain the only father and son ever to share a Nobel.)

Tesla once predicted, "The household's daily newspaper will be printed 'wirelessly' in the home during the night." Maybe the Supreme Court should give the guy credit for the Internet, too.

Westinghouse, while Tesla can only lay claim to the eponymous minor rock band.

Conversation Starters

◆ By the age of five, young Tesla had already invented his own waterwheel and read the 100-volume set of the Complete Voltaire. By comparison, we could, um, count to 10 and pretty regularly avoid peeing on ourselves.

◆ Celibate throughout his life, Tesla also feared round objects (which perhaps goes along with the celibacy). He once said, "I do not think you can name many great inventions that have been made by the married man." The wedding ring, perhaps?

◆ Tesla would have been great fun at parties. At the Chicago Columbia Exposition of 1893, he sent 200,000 volts through his body to prove that electricity was safe. It was, although his hair stood on end for a week.

◆ One of Tesla's best friends was another great non-Nobel-winning genius who managed to fritter away lots of money: Mark Twain.

◆ Not one for modesty, Tesla often signed his name with the letters G.I., short for Great Inventor.

Mark Twain

Name-dropping: Samuel Clemens (pronunciation: like it's spelled) (1835–1910). Businessman, speculator, orator, publisher, and author whose work revolutionized American literature and whose jokes are as funny today as they were 150 years ago.

When to Drop Your Knowledge: Quoting Twain will make you seem funny *and* smart. Below, we'll give you wry quotes on three popular small-talk topics: the weather, Congress, and the French.

The Basics

Samuel Clemens grew up in Hannibal, Missouri, on the banks of the Mississippi River. Both Hannibal and the Mighty Mississippi would play a profound role in his writing career. As a young man he worked as a steamboat captain on the river, a job he would recount with awe and love in his greatest nonfiction book, *Life on the Mississippi*. And Hannibal would serve as the model for Tom Sawyer and Huck Finn's hometown in Twain's best-remembered novels.

But Twain's writing career began in the wild American West. Having failed as a businessman (for the first of what would be many times), Twain began writing humorous sketches about the American West that captured dialect with his distinctly literal rendering of Americans' eccentric speechifying. The best of these, "The Celebrated Jumping Frog of

Caleveras County," made Twain a national celebrity (and, years later, would result in Calaveras High School picking the bullfrog as its mascot). His early career was marked by light and exceedingly funny writings—the Bill Bryson of his day, he got rich off humorous travelogues like *Roughing It* and *The Innocents Abroad*. And while these books were ostensibly nonfiction, Twain never had a problem stretching the truth—he once claimed, for instance, that the Egyptians used mummies to power their locomotives. Late in his career, however, Twain's work (although still funny) became darker and increasingly bitter, vociferously attacking religion and the injustices within American society.

Twain was perched between the light and dark phases of his career when he wrote his best book, *The Adventures of Huckleberry*

Bad Books

Twain was perhaps more inconsistent than any other major American author. Even his masterpiece, *The Adventures of Huckleberry Finn*, is often criticized for its last third, when the book veers from its compelling themes of conscience, racism, and nationalism, and becomes mere shenanigans. Some of his books *were* consistent— consistently awful. Among the ones you don't see in book stores much anymore:

- Two sequels to *Tom Sawyer*: *Tom Sawyer Abroad* and *Tom Sawyer, Detective*.
- *Christian Science,* a relentless, hilarious, and somewhat misogynistic attack on the religion and its founder, Mary Baker Eddy.
- *1601*, a sort of pauper's *The Prince and the Pauper*, without the good plot.
- And, of course, *A Dog's Tale*, in which Twain fell into the all-too-common trap of telling a story from a dog's perspective.

COCKTAIL PARTY CHEAT SHEETS

Quotable Twain

Presaging contemporary American opinions of France: "France had neither winter nor summer nor morals—apart from these drawbacks it is a fine country."

Presaging the banning of: "First God created idiots. That was just for practice. Then He created school boards."

On weather: "Climate is what we expect; weather is what we get." (**Note:** Twain never said, "Everyone talks about the weather, but no one ever does anything about it." That's a misattribution.)

On Congress: "It could probably be shown by facts and figures that there is no distinctly native criminal class except Congress."

Finn. Originally published for adolescents, *Huck Finn* is at once a classic adventure story, a hilarious introduction to the many characters of the river, and a superb attack on the racist and class-dominated social order of the day. The only knock on Twain is that he never wrote another *Huck Finn*. But to paraphrase Joseph Heller: If Twain never wrote anything like *Huck Finn* ever again, well—neither did anyone else.

THE HIGHEST PRAISE

Among Twain's biggest fans are many of the American authors who came after him. Faulkner called him "the first truly American writer." And Ernest Hemingway, in particular, admired Twain. He once said, "All modern American literature comes from one book by Mark Twain called *Huckleberry Finn*. . . . There was nothing before.[1] There has been nothing as good since." That last sentence means a lot coming from Hemingway, because he fancied himself awfully, awfully good.

[1] Sorry, Nathaniel Hawthorne.

Conversation Starters

◆ Most of us know that Samuel Clemens is generally believed to have picked the pen name Mark Twain, which he first used when he was 27, as a reference to Mississippi riverboat captain slang for "two fathoms deep" (thus, just barely navigable). But some students of Twain argue for an alternate theory: When he first used the name in his wild days in the West, they argue, he would stop in at a saloon, buy two drinks, and tell the bartender to "mark twain" on his tab.

◆ Twain was born in 1835, a year when Halley's comet was visible from Earth. In 1909, he wrote, "I came in with Halley's Comet . . . and I expect to go out with it." Indeed, he did. When he died on April 21, 1910, the comet was still visible in the night sky.

◆ Although Twain professed to hate captains of industry, it was an executive from Standard Oil, Henry H. Rogers, who helped Twain organize his finances toward the end of Twain's life. The two became great friends, and one might accuse Twain of hypocrisy, except Rogers was no ordinary industrialist: Although he was nicknamed "Hellhound Rogers" for his hard-nosed business deals, he was a secret softy. Rogers helped pay for the schooling of Helen Keller, quietly helped build elementary schools for African Americans in the South, and helped fund Booker T. Washington's Tuskegee Institute.

♷ Ulysses: The Book

- **Name-dropping:** James (pronunciation: like LeBron) Joyce (pronunciation: like Brothers) (1882–1941). Irish writer, widely considered the best novelist of the 20th century, whose magnum opus *Ulysses* brought modernism in literature to the forefront and became an instant literary classic, even though it's well known that about 11 people in all of human history have read it. Fortunately for you, your friends at **mental**_floss are among those 11, and we aim to spare you the trouble.
- **When to Drop Your Knowledge:** Bibliophiles everywhere will find your knowledge of *Ulysses* both enchanting and intimidating, and you can speak with authority about it, because—in all likelihood—they haven't read it either.

The Basics

James Joyce once wrote of *Ulysses,* "I've put in so many enigmas and puzzles that it will keep the professors busy for centuries arguing over what I meant." Mission accomplished. In 2000, *Ulysses* was hailed by the Modern Language Association as the greatest novel of the 20th century, but not everyone can even agree that it *is* a novel. It is, regardless, hilarious and self-referential and dazzlingly, ostentatiously brilliant—but most of all, it is extraordinarily difficult to read.

And yet, the plot is quite simple. Two men—a Jewish adman named Leopold Bloom and a young man with writerly

The Quotable Ulysses

Ulysses really is worth reading if you can find the time and summon the dedication. But if you can't, you can—like many millions before you—just *pretend* to have read it. Memorize these three quotes and you should be fine.

If someone says that *Ulysses* is a tough read, you say: "Indeed it is. I laughed out loud when I read 'I fear those big words,' Stephen said, which make us so unhappy.'"

If someone is talking about the themes of *Ulysses*, you say: "My favorite line is 'History, said Stephen, is a nightmare from which I am trying to awake.'"

And finally, if someone points out that you've just said something ridiculously untrue about *Ulysses*, you say: "A man of genius makes no mistakes. His errors are volitional and the portals to discovery."

aspirations named Stephen Dedalus—walk around Dublin, together and apart, on June 16, 1904. That's it. Not much happens: Stephen teaches some bored kids English; a fellow is buried; Bloom goes to a bar; Bloom and Stephen go to a brothel but don't hire anyone, etc. Told from a dizzying array of perspectives, often in the best stream-of-consciousness prose ever produced, *Ulysses* is much more than what happens. It's a perverted retelling of the *Odyssey*, a meditation on human consciousness, an exploration of nationalism, and an annoyingly punny comic novel ("Come forth, Lazarus! And he came fifth and lost the job").

It took Joyce seven years to write *Ulysses*, which he composed primarily while living in exile in Zurich and Trieste. But you wouldn't know he was a decade removed from life in Dublin to read the novel—Joyce

Bloomsday

Every June 16, literary nerds across the world band together to celebrate Bloomsday, an annual celebration of all things *Ulysses*. Readings are staged, academics present papers at conferences, and Dublin hosts marathon pub crawls. (Well, that happens on a lot of other days, too, but you get our drift.) In 2004, the 100th anniversary of Bloom's exploits, the city of Dublin served 10,000 visitors a free breakfast on Dublin's main thoroughfare, O'Connell Street.

imagined 1904 Dublin so perfectly that you could for many years precisely retrace Bloom's steps.

A VERY FORWARD FOREWORD

After a magazine serialized a chapter from *Ulysses* featuring masturbation, that chapter (and then the entire book) was declared obscene and banned from the U.S. A trial finally ensued in 1933 (which had a great title: "United States v. One Book Called *Ulysses*"). In the end, Judge John M. Woolsey ruled that the book was not obscene but was in fact "an amazing tour de force." Woolsey should have been a book reviewer! Joyce was so impressed with Woolsey's cogent, well-written judgment that Joyce insisted it be published as a kind of foreword to the book in the United States.

Conversation Starters

◆ When a young James Joyce and an aging W. B. Yeats (the two literary titans of 20th-century Ireland) first met, Joyce was stunningly pretentious. "We have met too late," Joyce told Yeats. "You are too old for me to have any effect on you."

◆ Joyce could have a sense of humor in conversation. When a young fan approached Joyce and asked if he could "kiss the hand that wrote *Ulysses*," Joyce replied, "No. It did lots of other things, too."

◆ The final chapter of *Ulysses* contains only eight sentences, though it is dozens of pages long (also, the chapter features no commas). Narrated in a stream of consciousness by Bloom's wife, Molly, the longest sentence in the chapter (known as "Penelope") is 4,391 words long. It held the record as longest sentence in a published novel from *Ulysses*'s publication in 1922 until 2001, when Jonathan Coe's *The Rotter's Club*, containing a 13,950-word sentence, was published.

◆ Joyce chose June 16, 1904, not for some complicated, metaphorically resonant reason, but because it was on June 16, 1904, that he and Nora Barnacle—who would later become his wife—went on their first date.

Ulysses: The Guy

Name-dropping: Odysseus (pronunciation: oh-DISS-ee-uss). Figure in Greek mythology most famously immortalized by the blind (and possibly nonexistent) Greek poet Homer. Builder of horses, husband of hotties, and extraordinary traveler, Odysseus is the epic hero par excellence.

Ulysses: Odysseus's name in Latin.

When to Drop Your Knowledge: The Ulyssesian hero has become so common that you're sure to find a way to work him in somewhere. Whether it's a discussion of *Finding Nemo*, Kerouac's *On the Road*, or *O Brother Where Art Thou?*, parallels abound. Plus, when you, the designated driver, leave the party to get more beer, you won't just be headed to the 7-Eleven anymore—you'll be embarking upon an *odyssey*.

The Basics

Smart, resourceful, and courageous, Odysseus is *the* epic hero (sorry, Achilles, but you have a heel and Odysseus doesn't). His story—and everything about Odysseus is mere story, since unlike other heroes of epic poems he never existed—begins during the Trojan War, when the wily Odysseus said (we are paraphrasing): "What if we built a Trojan horse and then when they look the gift horse in the mouth we attack?!" Which is what they did, and the Battle for Troy was won.

The Multifaceted Ulysses

Ulysses has proven such a fascinating and versatile character that he has appeared countless times in art. A few of his best appearances during his 2,500-year career were in:

- Greek tragedies by Sophocles and Euripides
- Virgil's *Aeneid*.
- Ovid's poems
- Dante's *Inferno*
- Shakespeare's *Troilus and Cressida*
- Alfred Lord Tennyson's poem *Ulysses*
- and, perhaps most important, in the 1981 anime classic *Ulysses 31,* in which a 31st-century Ulysses must travel through space in search of the kingdom of Hades.

The Trojan horse would have made a fine end to a lesser story, but Odysseus's battles, as told in the *Odyssey*, were only beginning. For the next two years, the sailor and his men hopped from island to island and challenge to challenge. They ate locusts with the Locust Eaters, looted the city of Ciconia, killed a Cyclops who happened to be kin to the sea god Neptune, briefly got turned into pigs, and ventured into the Under-world. Then Odysseus washed ashore on a magical island inhabited by a nymph named Calypso, whereupon he cheated on his wife (against his will, of course! She had a mysterious power, this Calypso) for seven years.

It was not until Zeus himself told Calypso to let Odysseus be that the great and cunning warrior finally returned home to Ithaca, where his gorgeous wife, Penelope, had been fending off suitors for nearly a decade. Odysseus then showed the kind of level-headed nature common to epic heroes and action movie protagonists by killing all of Penelope's suitors in a fast-paced bow-and-arrow battle. For 2,500-year-old stuff, the story of

Seeking Homer

Did Homer exist? No one knows, but scholars still manage to fight about it. Some maintain that the same person wrote the *Iliad* and the *Odyssey*; others claim that it was two distinct poets from the same school of poetry. Either way, many academics believe that the epics were created by countless storytellers over centuries before finally being written down. And as the literary paper titled "Homer—Who Was She?" proves, some scholars also argue that Homer was a woman.

Odysseus/Ulysses is an action-packed thrill ride.

And that, in part, explains Ulysses's continuing significance. His character—clever, hardworking, dedicated, and just unlucky enough to find himself in fascinating scrapes—has proved as durable as the *odyssey*, a word we had to take from Homer because he captured it so perfectly.

SEPARATED AT BIRTH?

Ulysses	Ulysses S. Grant
Uncommonly talented military general	Uncommonly talented military general
Name was originally not Ulysses (Odysseus—changed because of Latin's popularity)	Name was originally not Ulysses (Hiram—changed because it was so lame)
Once got a Cyclops exceedingly drunk	Frequently got himself exceedingly drunk

Conversation Starters

◆ The full name of Ulysses in the original Greek is Odysseus Laertiades, which literally means "Odysseus, the Son of Laertes." But in later Greek sources, Odysseus's father was often identified as Sisyphus, the crafty murderer who got his comeuppance when he had to spend all eternity in Hades pushing a rock up a hill.

◆ One thing's for sure: The *Odyssey* wasn't written by noted American intellectual Homer Simpson, nor was he named for the poet. Despite rumors to the contrary, Homer was also not named for the character "Homer Simpson" in Nathanael West's 1939 novel *The Day of the Locust*. The truth is Homer Simpson is named Homer because Homer was the name of *Simpsons*'s creator Matt Groening's father. Poor Homer Groening. D'oh-ing from the grave, we're sure.

◆ The *Odyssey* wasn't originally a text—it was a memorized poem recited by bands of actors who spoke an amalgamated language. So, if Homer existed, he didn't just create the two greatest epics of all time in the *Iliad* and the *Odyssey*. He also created an entire dialect. Homeric Greek, which is distinct from all other forms of ancient Greek, mixed together several dialects to produce the language Homer thought superior.

Voltaire

Name-dropping: Voltaire (pronunciation: vol-TARE) (1694–1778). Writer, philosopher, and stalwart representative of the Enlightenment in Europe.

When to Drop Your Knowledge: Voltaire lends himself to a number of conversational topics: reason, promiscuity, Deism, the surprising attractiveness of female mathematicians, and the rights of those accused of crimes. This is the great joy of getting to know a multifaceted famous person.

The Basics

Although widely considered to be among the greatest French writers ever, very little of Voltaire's work is read today. Voltaire was born François-Marie Arouet (why he picked the pen name Voltaire is an enduring mystery) into a middle-class family. Initially, Voltaire gained prominence as sort of the Dorothy Parker of 18th-century France. His aphorisms (e.g., "Common sense is not so common") were widely quoted, but he wanted more.

Never a terribly modest man ("Paradise is where I am," he once noted), the young Voltaire wanted to be France's Virgil, an epic poet who would reinvigorate French intellectualism. Unfortunately, Voltaire wasn't that great a poet. His one epic poem, *Henriade*, reads like someone competing for an award for Worst Imitation of Virgil.

Mme du Châtelet

Voltaire had many, many affairs, but Mme du Châtelet was the love of his life. And no wonder. While most women of her generation were demure homebodies, Mme du Châtelet was a mathematician and physicist. After meeting Voltaire, she endeavored to learn English so she could translate Newton's *The Mathematical Principles of Natural Philosophy* into French, hoping that it might bring about a move toward reason and scientific exploration. She died in 1749, and it was seven more years before her translation of Newton began to be published. Amazingly, however, it did indeed lead to a reinvigorated interest in scientific study, bolstering the Enlightenment ideals she and Voltaire both cherished.

Then he got thrown into the Bastille after an argument with a nobleman who'd made fun of the name Voltaire. (Really.) The next decades of his life were spent in periodic exile, as Voltaire began writing plays and history that openly criticized the irrational and outmoded morality of Church and government alike.

In 1734, Voltaire met the love of his life, Gabrielle-Émilie Le Tonnelier de Breteuil, marquise du Châtelet, who unfortunately was married, but fortunately was married to a guy who didn't seem to care that she spent all her time with Voltaire. Their love affair lasted 15 years, until Châtelet's death during childbirth. (See sidebar.) Not until he was 64 did he write the Enlightenment classic *Candide,* a long short story detailing the sad life of a young philosopher who finally realizes the only way to happiness is "to cultivate one's own garden." This commonsense, nonidealized construction of happiness became identified forever after with Voltaire.

His other central contribution also came late in life. After

God Bless 'Em

After Voltaire purchased his estate at Ferney, he rebuilt the church there, and wasn't bashful about it. Above the church door read the inscription "Deo Erexit VOLTAIRE" ("Erected to God by Voltaire"), which was blasphemous if only because Voltaire made his own name so much bigger than God's. Even though Voltaire wrote extensively about the irrationality and dangers of the Church (and publicly stated that he didn't believe Jesus ever existed), he somehow convinced the pope himself to send him a relic—that is, a piece of a dead saint's body—to sanctify Voltaire's crazy church.

he retired to a large estate in the town of Ferney, Voltaire began more actively crusading against oppression and bigotry. His writings advocated religious tolerance, the abolition of torture, and civil rights of commoners. It was in these liberal polemics, almost all of them written when he was an old man, that he truly established his lasting reputation.

SEPARATED AT BIRTH?

Voltaire	Madonna
Known for his willingness to sleep with most anybody	Known for her willingness to sleep with most anybody
Known by only one name	Known by only one name
Sacrilegious	Sacrilegious
Spent some time chained up in the Bastille	Spent some time chained up during photo shoots for her book *Sex*

Conversation Starters

◆ Although Voltaire came from a fairly well-off family, he didn't become really rich until he played the lottery. In 1728, a friend of Voltaire's noticed that the French government had accidentally created a lottery in which the prize money was significantly larger than the cost of all the tickets combined. So Voltaire formed a syndicate, bought all the tickets and won the lottery.

◆ Voltaire had many hated rivals, but he reviled no man quite so much as Élie-Catherine Fréron, a journalist who attacked the ideas of the Enlightenment and savagely panned one of Voltaire's plays (Fréron was right on that count—the play was horrible). Voltaire disliked Fréron so deeply that he had a painting of Fréron displayed in his dining room at Ferney. Of course, the portrait was no ordinary pic: It featured a terrified Fréron getting whipped by a band of demons.

◆ Like a lot of intellectuals who'd come after him, Voltaire loved coffee—*really, really* loved it, to the tune of a purported 50 cups a day (the cups were smaller than today's uber-grande lattes, but still!). So the next time someone says coffee is bad for you, point out that, in an era when popular treatments for disease included leeches and "quieting the nervous energy," Voltaire lived to the ripe old age of 83.

Virginia Woolf

- **Name-dropping:** Virginia Woolf (pronunciation: like the state, like the animal) (1882–1941). One of Britain's most important novelists, critics, and major modernist authors. She was also played in the film *The Hours* by Nicole Kidman, who won an Oscar primarily for wearing a fake nose. Where's Groucho Marx's Oscar?! But we digress.
- **When to Drop Your Knowledge:** Ms. Woolf's tragic life story will be helpful if you ever have to talk a cocktail party companion down off the edge of a roof deck, for sure. But she'll also be extremely helpful to you when you're chatting up a gender studies major and get called upon to prove your feminist chops. (That goes for you, too, boys; feminism isn't just for the ladies anymore.)

The Basics

Woolf grew up in an intellectual family, but didn't begin writing books until she was in her 30s, after she'd married Leonard Woolf and founded the Hogarth Press. Virginia's first two novels, while excellent, were stylistically traditional. But after World War I, she began to experiment, especially with the idea of time and conceptions of gender—themes that would become central to the modernist movement that she helped spearhead.

To the Lighthouse and *Mrs. Dalloway* are perhaps Woolf's

Drowning Poetic

While it's more or less par for the course for poets to die tragically, a surprisingly large percentage of them end up literally drowning their sorrows. Besides Woolf:

Percy Bysshe Shelley. The Romantic poet drowned in a mysterious boating accident on July 8, 1822. Rumors have swirled ever since that it was suicide.

Hart Crane. Perhaps tired of being known as the third-best American poet of his time (behind e.e. cummings and T. S. Eliot), in 1932, he said, "Good-bye, everybody!" and then leapt from the deck of a cruise ship. His body was never found.

Li Po. The best poet in eighth-century China, Li Po purportedly drowned while drunkenly trying to embrace the reflection of the moon in the Yangtze River.

most famous novels. Massively introspective, discursive, and stylistically challenging, *To the Lighthouse* might not be the book to take with you to the beach. As in many great literary novels, what happens (the Ramsey family, over the course of several years, finally arrives at a lighthouse) takes a backseat to the brilliance of the story's telling and the entrancing complexities of Woolf's language. For instance: Time passes in inverse proportion to the number of words in each section, a kind of novelistic interpretation of Einsteinian relativity.

Woolf was also a vitally important force in 20th-century feminism. Her nonfiction book *A Room of One's Own* remains the greatest description of the difficulties a female writer faces. She famously argued that to make one's way in the literary world, one needed only 50 pounds a month and a room of her own.

Woolf's literary importance can hardly be overstated. Along

with writers like James Joyce (see p. 164), she argued that literature could no longer ignore the inner workings of characters' lives but instead had to confront the complexity of being human head-on.

The complexity of Woolf's humanity, sadly, met an unfortunate end. She was plagued throughout her life with periods of insufferable depression. In 1941, Woolf wrote a heartbreaking suicide note to her husband, filled her pockets with stones, and drowned herself in the River Ouse. Although the marriages of major writers have often been marked by neglect, infidelity, and general misery, Virginia and Leonard had a remarkably loving relationship. In her suicide note, she wrote, "I feel certain that I am going mad again. I feel we can't go through another of those terrible times. And I shan't recover this time. I begin to hear voices, and can't concentrate. So I am doing what seems the best thing to do." For her, perhaps. But for the rest of us, losing whatever writing Woolf had before her was definitely not the best thing.

Conversation Starters

◆ While there's no question that the work of James Joyce influenced Woolf's *Mrs. Dalloway*, Woolf held a generally low opinion of Joyce and thought him a misogynist.

◆ As a child, Woolf and her sister, Vanessa (who became a prominent interior designer), were sexually abused by their half-brothers. Courageously, Woolf wrote of the abuse openly and without shame in her short memoir *Moments of Being*.

◆ Sister Vanessa, incidentally, was engaged in a very odd love quadrangle. Vanessa had an open marriage with British critic Clive Bell. She ended up having an affair with the bisexual painter Duncan Grant. Together, they had a daughter, Angelica, who ended up marrying Grant's one-time male lover, the British writer David Garnett.

◆ Grant, Garnett, Vanessa Bell, and Virginia Woolf were all members of the loose association known as the Bloomsbury Group, so called because they would hang out together in fancy houses in the Bloomsbury section of London. The Bloomsburies also included novelist E. M. Forster and economist John Maynard Keynes (see p. 90).

◆ Although we liked *The Hours* and enjoy a good cry as much as anyone, Woolf scholars were notably displeased with her portrayal in both the book and the movie. Many felt that novelist Michael Cunningham completely misrepresented Woolf, with one Woolf biographer going so far as to say that the film version "evacuates her life of political intelligence or social acumen" and reduces her to a "doomed, fey, mad victim." Burn. (*The Hours*, incidentally, was Woolf's working title for the novel that became *Mrs. Dalloway*.)

About the Editors

Will Pearson and **Mangesh Hattikudur** met as freshmen at Duke University, and in their senior year parlayed their cafeteria conversations into the first issue of *mental_floss* magazine. Five years later, they're well on their way to creating a knowledge empire. In addition to the magazine, a board game, a weekly CNN *Headline News* segment, and four *mental_floss* books, Will and Mangesh coauthored a novel, *Ulysses,* which was published under the pseudonym James Joyce.

John Green is the author of the critically acclaimed novel *Looking for Alaska* (2005), which has been translated into eight languages and is being made into a film by Paramount Pictures. John also contributes commentary to NPR's *All Things Considered.* A longtime fan of cocktail parties, he can generally be found at the buffet table, where his favorite topics of conversations are (1) the love lives of various historical figures and (2) why no one ever serves beans & weenies anymore. What's so wrong with beans & weenies? Enough with the brie and fancy crackers already. A buffet table is no place for pretension.

A Genius for Every Occasion . . .

mental_floss Cocktail Party Cheat Sheets
0-06-088251-4 (paperback)
Available 6/06
Don't be a wallflower at your next social outing, just fake your way through the conversation! These cheat sheets will have you equipped to handle the brainiest of topics in no time.

mental_floss Scatterbrained
0-06-088250-6 (paperback)
Available 8/06
Based on *mental_floss* magazine's popular "Scatterbrained" section, this book features thousands of juicy facts and tantalizing bits of trivia that are connected humorously—from Greece (the country) to *Grease* (the movie) to greasy foods and on and on.

mental_floss What's the Difference?
0-06-088249-2 (paperback)
Available 8/06
Want to spot a Monet from a Manet, kung fu from karate, or Venus from Serena Williams? Piece of cake! Whether you're trying to impress your boss, mother-in-law, attractive singles, or your 4th grade teachers, *mental_floss* has hundreds of quick tricks to make you sound like a genius.

mental_floss Genius Instruction Manual
0-06-088253-0 (paperback)
Available 11/06
The Genius Instruction Manual is the ultimate crash course on how to talk, act, and even dress like a genius. Presented by the brainiac team at *mental_floss*, it's the one stop shop for today's impossibly clever, cultured and sophisticated person.

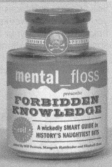

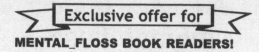

CPSIA information can be obtained
at www.ICGtesting.com
Printed in the USA
LVHW032015170322
713623LV00015B/542

9 780060 882518